GOLDEN BATS
AND
PINK PIGEONS

Gerald Durrell

summersdale

GOLDEN BATS AND PINK PIGEONS

First published in the UK by Collins in 1977
Previously published by Fontana 1979 and HarperCollins in 1996

This edition published by Summersdale Publishers Ltd. 2007

Illustrations by Edward Mortelmans

Reprinted 2008

Summersdale Publishers Ltd
46 West Street
Chichester
West Sussex
PO19 1RP
UK

www.summersdale.com

Printed and bound in India.

ISBN: 1-84024-635-9
ISBN 13: 978-1-84024-635-3

This is for Farida and Wahab
whose kindness and hospitality
sum up the whole charm of
Mauritius

CONTENTS

FOREWORD

by Lee Durrell

It's no wonder that Mauritius attracted Gerald Durrell like a magnet. It was the home of that large flightless bird, the dodo, the definitive symbol of extinction. Gerry had established his animal sanctuary in Jersey, now called the Durrell Wildlife Conservation Trust or 'Durrell' for short, to turn the tide of species extinctions. He started by breeding rare animals so that their kind were not lost forever, but in time he focussed on ensuring the survival of certain key species in the wild.

The Mascarenes, a complex of islands in the western Indian Ocean, including Mauritius, its offshore islets and Rodrigues, were the scene of the Trust's first sustained overseas conservation efforts, where the initial steps were taken with the ultimate goal in sight. *Golden Bats and Pink Pigeons* records the highlights of this journey, often hilarious, sometimes moving, and animated with great characters, both human and non-human, always described in Gerry's inimitable style.

Gerry and his assistant, John Hartley (later to become the Trust's Conservation Programme Director), set out to learn for themselves the plight of various creatures unique to the islands – from the snakes and lizards of Round Island, to the fruit bats of Rodrigues, to the pigeons and kestrels of Mauritius itself

– and to see what could be done to save them. The strategy involved setting up breeding programmes not only in Jersey, but also in Mauritius, at a facility which is now named the Gerald Durrell Endemic Wildlife Sanctuary.

Gerry wanted the first ever student at the Trust's training centre to come from the land of the dodo, so he was on the lookout for promising candidates during those early trips. In fact, the training centre was only a twinkle in his eye at that point, but he had long been convinced that the breeding of endangered species should be done in the country of origin of the species concerned. Thus he intended for the animal sanctuary in Jersey to become a 'mini-university' for conservation, whose graduates would return to their homes and put what they had learned into practice.

Mauritius, not surprisingly, is the scene of our first unequivocal conservation successes. The work started by Gerry and John some thirty years ago evolved into full-scale species recovery programmes, and now Durrell is credited with saving more species of bird from extinction than any other organisation.

You will read more about these achievements in the excellent afterword by Toni Hickey, Senior Bird Keeper at Durrell, which brings me neatly to my final thought here. It is about the remarkable commitment and selfless hard work that our staff, like Toni and her colleagues, undertake to follow Gerald Durrell's dream.

These men and women, plus the graduates of our International Training Centre – yes, Gerry did indeed set up his training centre – are collectively referred to as Durrell's.

A WORD IN ADVANCE

I think a brief explanation of this book is called for. It describes two separate trips that I, my assistant John Hartley and my secretary Ann Peters made to the enchanting island of Mauritius. My reasons for going there were twofold.

I established the Jersey Wildlife Preservation Trust some years ago to help endangered species by breeding them in captivity. This we have done with great success, but it became obvious to me that really the animals in question should be bred in their country of origin. The problem was that in most of these countries there were no personnel trained in the delicate art of wild animal husbandry. The trust, therefore, set up a scholarship scheme whereby we give financial assistance to students to come to us for training and then return to their countries to set up captive breeding programmes. To inaugurate the scholarship scheme, as the Dodo was our symbol, it seemed appropriate that a Mauritian student should be the first to benefit. I therefore went out to discuss this whole business with the Mauritian Government. At the same time, I wished to see some of the endangered birds, mammals and reptiles and to find out if we could in any way help the Mauritian Government in their efforts to save them. This is the story of how we set about it.

A WORD IN ADVANCE

CHAPTER ONE

MACABEE AND
THE DODO TREE

When you are venturing into a new area of the world for the first time, it is essential – especially if you are an animal collector – that you do two things. One is to get as many personal introductions as you can to people on the spot; the second to amass as much information as possible, no matter how esoteric or apparently useless, about the place that you are going to. One of the ways you accomplish this latter is by contacting the London Embassy or High Commission of the country concerned. In many cases, this yields excellent results and you are inundated with maps and vividly coloured literature containing many interesting facts and much misinformation. In other cases, the response is not quite so uplifting. I am, for example, still waiting for all the information promised me by a charming Malay gentleman in the London High Commission when I was going to that country. My trip there was eight years ago. However, the response you get from the Embassy or High Commission generally gives you some sort of a clue as to the general attitude prevailing towards life in the country concerned.

Bearing this in mind, I hopefully rang up the Mauritian High Commission in London when it was finally decided we were going there. The phone was answered by a charming young lady with a most attractive Asian accent.

'Hallo,' she said, with interest, but cautiously, not divulging her phone number or identity.

'Is that the Mauritian High Commission?' I asked.

'Yes,' she admitted at last, rather reluctantly, 'that's right.'

'The Mauritian High Commission?' I repeated, making sure.

'Yes,' she said, more certainly this time, 'Mauritian.'

'Oh, good.' I said, 'I was hoping you could give me some information as I am very much hoping to go there soon.'

'Go *where*?' she asked at length.

I knew that Mauritius was fairly remote but this, I felt, was too much. However, this was my first introduction to the charming illogicality of the Mauritian way of life. Eventually I did receive from the High Commission a small booklet containing, amongst other things, slightly out-of-focus pictures of Miss Mauritius 1967 lying about on beaches which could have been situated in Bognor or Bournemouth, for all the evidence to the contrary. Reluctantly I went back to the books of the early naturalists and more up-to-date zoological and geographical tomes for my information.

The Mascarene Islands, of which Mauritius is the second largest, lie embedded in the Indian Ocean, east of Madagascar. Forty miles by twenty, Mauritius gleams in a million tropical greens, from the greens of dragon wing and emerald, to delicate dawn greens and the creamy greens of bamboo shoot. All this is encrusted with a rainbow of flowers from the great trees that flame like magic bonfires of fragile violet-shaped magenta blooms, lying like a thousand shed butterfly wings among the grass, which itself can be green or yellow, or as pink as the sunset.

In the dawn of the world, Mauritius was formed – when the great volcano pustules were still bursting and spilling out fire and lava. In a series of cataclysmic convulsions, the island was wrenched from the sea bed and lifted skywards, the hot rocks glowing and melting so that cyclone and tidal wave, hot wind and great rains, moulded and fretted it, and tremendous earth shudders shook it and lifted it into strange mountain ranges, churning the tender rocks as a chef whips egg whites until they become stiff and form weird peaks when lifted up on a fork tip. So the strange-shaped mountains of Mauritius grew; miniature mountains all under 3,000 feet, but as distinctive, unique and Daliesque, as if carefully designed for a stage back-drop. A multitude of coral polyps, as numerous as stars, then formed a protecting roof round it and contained the lagoon, which encircled the island as a moat encircles a fortress.

Gradually, as the earth formed, seeds arrived, either sea or air-borne, to send their roots into the volcanic soil, now soft and rich, watered by many bright rivers. Following, came birds and bats carried by errant winds, tortoises and lizards like shipwrecked mariners on rafts of branches and creepers from other lands. These settled and prospered and gradually, over millions of years, their progeny evolved along their own lines, unique to the islands.

So the Dodo came into being; and the big, black, flightless parrot. The tortoises grew larger and larger until they were the size of an armchair and weighed over two thousand pounds, and the lizards vied with each other in evolving strange shapes and rainbow colours. There being no major predators except an owl and a small kestrel, the creatures evolved without defence. The Dodo became flightless, fat and waddling, nesting on the ground in safety, as did the parrot. There was nothing to harass the slow, antediluvian life of the tortoise; only the quick, glittering lizards and the golden-eyed geckos needed to fear the hawk and the owl.

There, on this speck of volcanic soil in the middle of a vast sea, a complete, unique and peaceful world was created slowly and carefully. It waited there for hundreds of thousands of years for an annihilating invasion of voracious animals for which it was totally unprepared, a cohort of rapacious beasts led by the worst predator in the world, *Homo sapiens*. With man, of course, came all his familiars: the dog, the rat, the pig, and, in this instance, probably one of the worst predators next to man, the monkey.

In an incredibly short space of time, a number of unique species had vanished – the Dodo; the giant, black, flightless parrot; the giant Mauritian tortoise, rapidly followed by the Rodrigues tortoise; and that strange bird, the Solitaire. The dugong, which used to throng the reefs, vanished and all that was left of a unique and harmless fauna was a handful of birds and lizards. These, together with what is left of the native forest, face enormous pressures. Not only is Mauritius one of the most densely populated parts of the globe, but as well as dogs, cats, rats and monkeys, a number of other things have been introduced in that dangerous, unthinking way that man has. There are, for example, 20 introduced species of bird, which include the ever-present house sparrow and the swaggering, dominating mynah. There is the sleek and deadly mongoose and less damaging but still out of place, the hedgehog-like tenrec from Madagascar. Then there are the introduced plants and trees, so that the native vegetation is jostled and strangled by Chinese guava, wild raspberries, privet and a host of other things. In the face of all this, the indigenous flora and fauna of Mauritius can be said to be hanging on to its existence by its finger nails.

In spite of my misgivings after my exchange with the High Commission, I found Mauritius, although indeed remote, was neither unknown nor inaccessible. Within a few days, Air France, who wonderfully stage-managed the entire trip, wafted us halfway across the world in the lap of luxury, our every want catered for by voluptuous air hostesses; so much so, that John Hartley and I felt we would be reluctant to leave the plane and brave the outside world again. But when the island came into view, we were seized with the excitement that always engulfs one when a new country suddenly presents itself to be explored. It lay, green and smouldering, mountains smudged blue and purple, like some monstrous precious stone in a butterfly-blue enamel setting, ringed with the white foamed reef and displayed, as a jewel is displayed on velvet, on the dark blue of the Indian Ocean. As our pachyderm aircraft lumbered in to land, we could see the green islets lying within the reef, star-white beaches and the square fields of sugar cane covering, it seemed, every available piece of flat land, lapping the base of the curiously shaped mountains like a green check tablecloth. It was somehow ironical that we, the flightless mammals, were landing, in one of the biggest flying edifices known on earth, on the area of land that covered the remains of one of the earth's strangest flightless birds; for the Dodo's graveyard, from which were extracted the bones on which our tenuous knowledge of the Dodo is based, lies beneath the tarmac of Plaisance airport.

The doors of the plane opened and we were lapped in the warm scented air and dazzled by the brilliance of colours that only the tropics can provide. In thick clothes – it had been snowing in England – one felt the sweat prickle out all over one's body and dribble in uncomfortable rivulets down one's back and chest. We were ushered through Customs with the minimum of fuss, thanks to the enchantingly charming gentleman with the euphonious name of Lee Espitalier Noel – there were, we discovered, over two hundred in the family which caused them to give up exchanging Christmas presents – who had a delicious French accent that would have made Maurice Chevalier sound Cockney.

It was here that we discovered one of the many incongruities of Mauritius. In an island that had been an English colony for over one hundred and fifty years and was still a member of the Commonwealth, where English was taught in schools as the official language, everyone gaily and volubly spoke French. We also found a strange amalgamation of the English and Gallic cultures; although traffic progressed on the left-hand side of the road and hand signals were correct and as graceful as a ballerina's dance movements, the driving was of the suicidal variety that the French nation delighted to indulge in.

Our Creole driver drove at a ferocious speed down the road lined with half-grown sugar cane, the stems of delicate pinky-blue and the leaves acid green, through villages of tin and wooden houses, thronged by groups of women, gay as butterflies in multi-coloured saris, surrounded by dogs, chickens, goats, humped-backed cattle and children in an exuberant melee. Each village was fragrant with the smells of fruit and flowers, alight with trailing shawls of bougainvillaea, each shaded by a giant banyan tree, like a hundred huge, black melted candles with green flames of leaves fused together in a mammoth, sheltering, shade-quivering bulk.

I was enchanted by the signs we passed – 'Mr Tin Win Wank' who was licensed to sell tobacco and spirits On and Off (the premises, one presumed, rather than as the spirit moved him); the mysterious signpost in the miles and miles of sugar cane that said, simply and unequivocably, 'Trespass', and as to whether this was a warning or invitation, there was no indication. When we slowed down for a group of grunting, fly-veiled pigs to cross the road, I was delighted to observe that the village contained a 'Mr Me Too', who was a watchmaker, and a 'Mr Gungadin', no less, who finding his premises at a crossroads had, with a flash of Asian originality, called his shop 'Gungadin Corner Shop'. This was to say nothing of the neat little notices everywhere in the cane fields under the banyan trees saying 'Bus Stop' or, on several occasions, ones adjuring you to 'Drive slowly School crossing'. In this Alice in Wonderland atmosphere one had a vision of a large wooden building on rollers, full of enchanting children, being drawn back and forth across the road. Other place names in Mauritius had fascinated me as I pored over the map before leaving, and now we passed through some of them.

Eventually, drugged by heat, jet-lag and all the tropical scents, dazzled by sun and colour, and terrified by our driver's ability to avoid death by inches, we arrived at the rambling, spacious hotel spread out in groves of hibiscus, bougainvillaea and casuarina trees along the blue and placid lagoon, with the strange mini-Matterhorn of Le Morne mountain looming up behind it. Here, we were greeted with gentle, languid charm and wafted to our respective rooms, thirty yards from where the blue sea whispered enticingly on the white beach.

The next day, we went down to meet the McKelveys of Black River, where the captive breeding programmes, sponsored by the International Council for Bird Preservation, the World Wildlife Fund and the New York Zoological Society, has been set up. David and his attractive wife, Linda, greeted us warmly and started telling us some of the trials and tribulations attendant upon trying to track down and capture specimens of the 33 Pink pigeons and the eight kestrels, which were the total population of these, some of the world's rarest birds, in a thickly forested area the size of Hampshire. That Dave had met with success at all, was a miracle. He was an attractive-looking man in his mid-thirties, with dark hair and blue eyes that beamed with enthusiasm. His somewhat nasal voice seemed just a shade too loud, as if pitched towards that section of the audience farthest back in the hall. He had that nimbleness of wit and phrase that makes the speech of humorous Americans among the funniest and raciest in the world. The rapid, wise-cracking speech, studded with superlatives like a Dalmatian with spots, was in Dave's case accompanied by the most extraordinary power of mimicry, so that he not only told you how the pigeons flew in overhead and landed and cooed, but imitated them so vividly that you felt you were witnessing the event.

'I walked in those goddarned woods looking for the roosting sites until I sure as hell felt like a water-shed, the way I was rained on. I thought maybe I would get to growing mushrooms between my toes as a sideline. I felt about as hopeful as if I was looking for Dodos. I used to stay up there until way after dark, and let me tell you, it's blacker than the inside of a dead musk ox's stomach on those hills after dark. Then one day, wham, there they all were, flying in to Cryptomeria Valley, their wings going "whoof, whoof, whoof" and then, when they settled, they kind of bowed to each other and then went "caroo, coo, coo, caroo, coo, coo".'

Dave burbled on in this vein as he led us from his house to the walled garden nearby, where an enthusiastic local aviculturalist had donated the aviary space for the project.

'Now,' said Dave, as he led us up to the first aviary, 'now you are going to see one of the rarest birds in the world and one of the most goddarned beautiful too, and tame as a newly-born guinea pig. They were from the start. There!'

In the aviary sat three undeniably handsome pigeons. They were much larger than I had imagined and more streamlined, but this was due to their extraordinary long tails and necks. With their reddish-brown plumage and the delicate cyclamen-pink blush on their necks and breasts, they were large and very elegant members of the family. They had small heads perched on long, soigné necks, which gave them a look rather like a feathered antelope. As we approached the wire, they peered at us in the mildly interested, oafish way that pigeons have and then, dismissing us from what passed for their minds, they fell into a doze. I felt that even though their rarity made them of great biological and avicultural importance, one could hardly say that they had personalities that inspired one.

'They look rather like a wood pigeon that has been dyed,' I said, unthinkingly, and Dave gave me a wounded look.

'There's only thirty-three of them left,' he said, as though this made them much more desirable and beautiful than if there had been 25 million.

We moved on to the aviary that contained a pair of Mauritian kestrels. They were small, compact birds with wild, fierce-looking eyes, but here again, they bore such a close resemblance to the European and North American kestrels that only an expert could tell them apart, and the uninitiated could well be pardoned for wondering what all the fuss was about. Was I, I wondered, being unfair to the Mauritian kestrel just because it closely resembled a bird that I had been familiar with from childhood, had kept and flown at sparrows? Did this make me less anxious to enthuse over it than if it had been something as bizarre as a Dodo? After mature reflection for at least thirty seconds, I decided that this was not the case. Nothing could be more boringly like a guinea pig than a West Indian hutia, a rodent to which I was passionately attached and whose future was as black as the kestrels'. No, it was simply that I was more mammal than bird-orientated, and so a small, dull mammal appealed to me more than a small, dull hawk. I decided that this was remiss of me and made a vow to make amends in the future. Dave, meanwhile, was regaling me with the fate of a pair of kestrels that had been foolish enough to nest on a cliff face that was not totally inaccessible.

'Monkeys,' said Dave, dramatically, 'the forest's full of the damn things. Big as a six-year-old child, some of the males. Travel in huge troops. You can hear them, "aaagh, aaagh, aaagh, eeek, eeek, eeek, yaah, yaah" (that's the old male), and then there are the babies, "week, week, week, eeek, eeek, eeek, yaah, yaah, yaah".'

A whole troop of malevolent monkeys, from grandfathers to newly born, were conjured up as a torrent of sound poured from Dave's vocal chords. These unnecessary, ingenious, and omnivorous pests had overrun the island and attacked not only the kestrels' nests but the Pink pigeons' as well.

After we had finished admiring the pigeons and the kestrels, we drove up to Curepipe, where the Forestry headquarters were situated. Here we met Wahab Owadally, the Conservator of Forests. He was a boyishly good-looking young Asian with an infectious grin and an even more infectious enthusiasm. After we had made polite noises at each other in his office, he and his European second-in-command, Tony Gardner, took us out to show us the handsome botanical garden that adjoined the office building. It was here that Wahab's enthusiasm completely changed my attitude towards palm trees. They had never seemed to me a very inspiring dendrological growth when seen, dusty and moulting, lining tropical streets or standing shivering in what passes for an English summer in places like Bournemouth or Torquay, but here in the spacious and beautifully laid-out grounds of the botanical gardens of Curepipe they had come into their own. There were the tall, elegant Hurricane palms, the Royal ones, with trunks like a piece of the Acropolis, the famous Coco de Mer from the Seychelles and, above all, the palms that went straight to my heart, the Bottle palms. Wahab introduced us (and I use the term advisedly) to a small plantation of these enchanting trees. The trunk of each baby palm was shaped just like a Chianti bottle and from the top, exuberant and uncombed, the fronds sprang out like a green fountain. They looked like strange pot-bellied people and when their fronds moved in the breeze, it seemed as if they were waving at you.

Back in Wahab's office, we discussed the things we ought to see and do in Mauritius. First of all, I was anxious to visit the Cryptomeria Grove in which the Pink pigeons nested, and then the Macabee Forest and the Black River Gorge Nature Reserves, which were the last haunt of the kestrel and the Mauritian parakeet. Wahab was also very insistent that we visit Round Island, a small island in a group lying north of Mauritius.

'It is Mauritius's answer to the Galapagos,' he said, grinning, 'an island of only three hundred and seventy-five acres, yet you have three species of tree, three species of lizard and two species of snake that are found nowhere else in the world. At the moment, the island is in great danger from introduced rabbits and goats, eating up all the vegetation. It's a desperate situation which I'll tell you more about when we are there. Until we solve this problem, the island is getting steadily more eroded so the reptile fauna is in great danger.'

'Does anyone know what the present population of these reptiles is?' I asked.

'Well,' said Wahab, pursing his lips, 'it's a bit difficult to get accurate figures but we reckon that Gunther's geckos and Telfair's skinks and Night geckos are probably down to five hundred or so. One snake, the Burrowing boa, has only been seen a few times in the last twenty years and is possibly extinct. The other, they reckon, is under seventy in number.'

'You ought to get some into captivity as a safeguard,' I suggested. Wahab's eyes gleamed.

'There's talk of a captive breeding programme. It was even suggested in the Proctor report, but so far no one has been willing to undertake it,' he said.

'I'll undertake it if you'll give me permission,' I said. 'We've just built a marvellous new Reptile Breeding Complex for this very kind of thing.'

'It will be excellent if you could,' said Wahab, as if the idea had only just occurred to him. 'How would you go about it?'

'Well let's do it in stages. If we get some of the more robust species first and meet with success with them, then next year, when I come out to help judge the candidates for the scholarship, we can get the other species. I would think we ought to start with the skinks and the Gunther's gecko which is a large, fairly tough thing, I imagine.'

'OK,' said Wahab, happily, 'I'll make arrangements for you to go to Round Island as soon as the weather is right. Meantime, Dave can show you the Macabee Forest.'

'Sure,' said Dave, 'I want to try and mist-net another kestrel, so that we can go and spend the day up there. We will take a couple of nets with my American kestrel as a lure, and try our luck. It's a lovely bit of country even if you don't catch anything. We can do that tomorrow, if you like.'

'And show him the Dodo tree,' said Wahab.

'What's a Dodo tree?' I asked.

'Wait and see,' said Wahab, mysteriously.

So, the following morning, we set out to spend the day in Macabee. To get to the Macabee Forest, you have to cross the Plains of Champagne, another evocative name. Here we stopped briefly to see some of the few remaining patches of native heath left in Mauritius; small, tough plants that form a unique ecological niche. It will be a pity to lose it. All over the world we are destroying forests and plant life generally with a profligacy that is incredible, for in our present state of knowledge we might well be destroying some species which might prove of enormous value to medicine.

Crossing the Plains of Champagne, with the scarlet and black Fodys perched like guardsmen in the heath or flying like scraps of fire across the road, we eventually entered a rough track like a ride in an English forest. This was the outskirts of Macabee. We drove for some way and then, in a clearing where the road split into four, Dave stopped the car and we got out. In the still, warm air, small flies hung like helicopters in the sun, their bodies golden green, their large eyes peacock blue. Occasionally, a chocolate-coloured butterfly would flap past in a tumble of wings like an old lady that was late for an appointment. On the ebony trees, tiny clusters of cream-coloured orchids clung, and everywhere there were the tall, slender, caramel and silver-green staves of the Chinese guava and little patches of privet, the pale and delicate green leaf edges of the young plants crinkled like a ballet skirt. It was warm and quiet and friendly. Here in these woods, there was nothing to harm you. The only seriously malign inhabitant was the scorpion, but in over fourteen weeks in Mauritius, during which I turned over stones, dissected rotting trees and rooted among fallen leaves like a truffle hound – the normal behaviour of a naturalist – I did not find one. Macabee was a friendly forest where you did not hesitate to sit down or lie down on the forest floor, secure in the knowledge that the only member of the local fauna likely to cause any trouble was the mosquito.

'Look there,' said Dave, 'now there's a sight for you, a phelsuma on a Dodo tree.'

He pointed to where a tall, silver-trunked tree grew at the side of the track. It was obviously old and in places it was starting to rot, for there were cracks in its buttress roots. It was some fifty feet high, ending in a tangle of branches and dark green leaves. On the trunk about six feet from the ground clung a breathtakingly beautiful lizard. It was some five inches long and the basic colouring was a bright, rich dragon green. On the head and neck, however, the colours merged into kingfisher blue with scarlet and cherry-red markings. It had large, intelligent, black eyes, and each of its toes was pressed out into a tiny pad, which gave it the suction necessary to cling to the smooth surface of the tree. We wanted to collect some of these beautiful day geckos, and so John had prepared our special lizard fishing rod which consisted of a long, slender bamboo with a fine nylon noose welded on to the end of it. Armed with this, he approached the phelsuma, which regarded him with an air of wide-eyed innocence. It let John get within six feet of the tree before it started to move, sliding gently over the bark as smoothly as a stone on ice. By the time John was close to the tree, the lizard was out of range some twenty feet up it and, for good measure, round the other side of the trunk.

'They are a bit wary here,' said Dave. 'I think it's because this road is used quite a bit. They are tamer farther into the forest, we should get some there.'

'Why do you call this the Dodo tree?' I asked.

'Ah,' said Dave, 'well, this is a tambalacoque tree, you see. It is one of the oldest of the Mauritian trees and there are only about twenty or thirty left. Now, this is the seed.'

He delved into his pocket and produced a curious-looking seed the size of a chestnut. It was pale biscuit brown and on one side it was fairly smooth, rather like a peach stone, while on the other it looked as though someone had started to carve it into an oriental face and had stopped halfway. The seed was quite heavy and obviously hard.

'Now,' said Dave, 'this is the theory and God knows who made it up, but it's a nice story. They've tried to germinate these seeds in various botanical gardens and at the Forestry Nursery but for some reason they can't grow the damn things. Now the tambalacoque was very common during the time of the Dodo and the theory goes that the Dodo liked to eat the fruit of the tree. As the flesh is digested, the gastric juices got to work on the hard seed and by the time the Dodo passed the seed out of its body, it was soft enough to germinate.'

'It's a lovely story,' I said, fascinated at the thought of such a link between a bird and a tree, and how the extermination of one was causing the disappearance of the other, 'but I'm afraid it's got more holes in it than a colander.'

'Yes,' said Dave, reluctantly, 'but it's a good story to tell the tourists and it is true that the tambalacoque is almost extinct.'

We made our way farther down into the forest, seeing the bright flash of phelsumas on nearly every tree trunk. The little golden greenflies hovered everywhere, some-times pursued by large pale-green dragonflies with crisp, transparent wings, and once a large stick insect blundered across the path, sealing-wax red and black, some eight inches long. Three or four times, mongooses – swift and deadly as arrows – sped across the ride ahead of us and once we rounded a corner and surprised a troop of monkeys who, like a conjuring trick, melted into the thick guava grove so rapidly you were almost uncertain that you had really seen them. Once, a flock of Ring-necked parakeets flew across the ride and away into the forest. They were a large proportion of the estimated fifty birds that were left. We stopped to admire a pair of the Mauritian merle, again a bird whose numbers are also declining with alarming speed. They are handsome birds with pleasant bubbling cries, and they evinced enormous curiosity at Dave's imitation of them, and came quite close, peering through the branches at us and 'chucking' in amazement to each other.

Presently we left the ride and followed the narrow forester's path that ran along the spine of a razor-backed ridge. The ground fell away sharply on each side of the trail, and between the trees we caught glimpses of the spectacular Black River gorges, thickly covered in forests of greens and reds and golds, with waterfalls like feathers trailing down the steep, spectacular cliff faces. At the bottom of the gorges, where the rivers ran bright and shining, or white and thunderous through mossy rock, the air was filled with drifting, wheeling, white crosses that were the White-tailed tropic birds. Soon we came to a place where a large, dead tree jutted out from the side of the path and overhung the valley far below, and it was here that Dave said he had seen Mauritian kestrels perch during their hunting sweeps through the gorges.

We unwrapped the mist nets and, with some difficulty, positioned them; then Dave unhooked the American kestrel and tethered her by her jesses to the branch of the dead tree. She bated a couple of times but soon settled down. We spread out along the path, concealed ourselves in the undergrowth and waited. I asked Dave, who had curled himself up into a bush quite close to me, who used these narrow paths that snaked through the forest, such as the one we were on. We had to be on the path for if you moved more than three feet either side you fell several hundred feet into the valley below, if not neatly spiked by guava trees on the way.

'They're forestry paths,' he said, 'but they're also used by the marijuana growers.'

'What marijuana growers?' asked Ann Peters, from her vantage point farther down the path.

'It's a flourishing business, growing pot,' David explained, 'they come into the forests and carve out a little garden, and then harvest the stuff and sell it '

'Isn't it illegal?' John asked.

'Of course,' said Dave. 'Mauritius has no army but they have what they call the Special Mobile Force, like the Marines or Commandos and one of their jobs is to hunt pot growers. They even do it by helicopter. I found a large garden a few weeks back and reported it to them. It was one of the largest hauls they'd had for a long time, so I guess that made me *persona non grata* with the drug boys for a time.'

The morning wore on and suddenly it was noon and the heat of the day. The sun burned down like the core of a furnace, and the forest was silent, lapped in heat. This was the time when nothing with any sense was abroad, so the kestrels would be wisely siesta-ing somewhere. We decided to have our lunch so we uncurled our cramped limbs and assembled on a moderately wide bit of path near the dead tree. Here, we spread out the food we had brought. We had just moved from sandwiches to some delicious mangoes, when two slender youths appeared walking towards us, dressed in multi-coloured shirts and flared trousers. Their shoulder-length hair, in a style which most Mauritian young men now favour, was black and glossy and framed incredibly handsome and gentle faces. They got to the point in the path where we and our picnic were presenting an obstacle, then came to a halt, smiling shyly and beguilingly.

'Good morning,' we said, politely.

'Good morning, Sir,' they chorused softly, raising their straw hats.

'You want to pass? Pass along,' said Dave, 'but don't step on me.'

'No, Sir,' they said, shocked at such a thought, and picked their way over our recumbent bodies and among our picnic things with the delicacy of a pair of gazelles. Having reached the other side without untoward incident, they said 'thank you, Sir, goodbye,' raised their hats again politely and set off down the path. Both of them, I noticed, carried machetes.

'Who on earth are they?' asked Ann.

'Well, they're not foresters,' said Dave, 'so they must be pot growers because, sure as hell, nobody but pot growers and lunatics like us are going to be out in the forest at this hour. I don't think they will be the only ones. I think "Mr Big" will probably be following.'

His prediction was right, for within five minutes another handsome, slender, deer-like Asian made his appearance. He had the indefinable something that stamped him as a lad from the big city. His suit was better cut and of better material, his shirt was more elegant, his hat more jaunty. He paused briefly and uncertainly when he saw us littering the path, then came on with an ingratiating smile.

'Good morning, Sir,' he said, all-embracingly doffing his hat, 'excuse me, but have you seen my friends?'

'Yes, two of them. They went that way,' said Dave, as if there was any choice. 'Do you want to pass?'

'Er... no, no,' said the young man. 'I must go and tell my other friend.'

'Ah, you have another friend?' said Dave.

'Yes,' said the young man, 'he is waiting back there. I must go and tell him which way my other friends go. Goodbye, Sir.'

'Goodbye,' we said, and watched him pick his way back along the path like an elegant, dusky ungulate.

'What was all that about?' asked John, puzzled.

'He's now gone back to warn the others,' said Dave, 'and they will get to the garden by the lower path. It is longer but it is a lot less risky as we are here.'

The afternoon wore on. It soon became obvious that we had little chance of catching a kestrel, so we dismantled the nets and Dave put the American kestrel on a stump nearby while we had some tea. Soon, to our astonishment, we descried 'Mr Big' himself approaching, but now from the opposite direction. As he reached us, it became obvious that during the course of the afternoon he had suffered a sea change. His hat was on the back of his head, his raven locks were dishevelled, and his eyes had the opaque, glazed look of one who has been suddenly woken from a deep sleep and has not quite bridged the gap between dreaming and reality. Though he still walked gracefully, he was more uncertain of his movements. When he reached us, he stopped and leaned negligently against a tree.

'Hello,' said Dave, 'have you had a nice walk?'

'Yes, I am walking,' 'Mr Big' explained, smiling benignly, 'I am walking in the forest.'

'Did you have a nice time?' asked Ann.

'Very nice, Madam,' he said, and went on to explain, 'I am walking for my health.'

We were a bit nonplussed by this, so said nothing. He gazed dreamily down into the wild vistas of the gorge, where the tropic birds whirled like snowflakes. He appeared to have forgotten our existence. His face had an expression of vacuous tranquillity on it. Suddenly, he came-to briefly.

'You are English?' he asked me.

'Yes,' I said.

'From London?' he asked.

'Thereabouts,' I said, not wanting to get bogged down in a lot of explanations as to where the Channel Islands were.

'I have many relatives in London,' he said, 'also many parents.'

'Really?' I said, fascinated.

'Many, many,' he said, 'I also have many parents and relatives in Birmingham.'

'A very nice place, Birmingham,' said John.

'Very nice, and London also. My parents say they are very nice, and...' he closed his eyes for a moment and I thought, like the dormouse in Alice, he had fallen asleep in mid-sentence. He suddenly opened his eyes, sighed deeply and continued, '... and I shall go there one day to join all my parents.'

'Do you often walk in the forest?' asked Dave.

'For my health, I often walk in the forest,' said 'Mr Big'.

'Do you ever see any birds?' asked Dave.

'Birds?' said 'Mr Big', examining the question. 'Birds? You are meaning birds?'

'Yes,' said Dave, 'you know, like pigeons or condé.'

'Birds?' said 'Mr Big'. 'Yes, sometimes I am seeing birds and sometimes hearing birds too, singing.'

'Do you ever see a small hawk, a kestrel?' asked Dave, 'the thing they call the "Mangeur de Poule"?'

'Mr Big' looked at Dave and then at the American kestrel, preening herself some three feet away. He closed his eyes briefly and licked his lips, then opened his eyes and looked at Dave and the kestrel again.

'Hawk?' he said, uncertainly.

'Yeah, we're looking for one,' Dave explained, oblivious.

'You are looking for a small hawk?' asked 'Mr Big', determined to get it right.

'Yes,' said Dave, 'the Mangeur de Poule.'

Again 'Mr Big' carefully examined Dave and the kestrel in close proximity. He closed his eyes again and then opened them, obviously hoping that the hawk could have vanished – it hadn't.

He was in a quandary. Was the hawk a figment of his marijuana-inflamed imagination? In which case, should he draw attention to it? If, on the other hand, it was real, why could not these people, who presumably had parents in London and Birmingham too, see the bird? The whole thing was very difficult, too difficult for him to manage. He gazed round desperately. We tried not to catch each others' eyes for fear of laughing. At last 'Mr Big' found the solution to the problem.

'Goodbye,' he said, and taking off his hat, he bowed, stepped over our recumbent forms and made his way uncertainly down the path.

An hour later, when we made our way down to the main ride, we suddenly came upon 'Mr Big' sitting on the ground with his back against a tree, reading a book and consuming a large sandwich.

'You have finished your walking?' he asked, jovially, getting to his feet and brushing some crumbs from his lap.

'Yes, we are going home now,' said Dave.

'To London?' asked 'Mr Big', surprised.

'No, Black River,' said Dave.

'Well, goodbye,' said 'Mr Big', 'I must be waiting for my friends.'

We got into the car and 'Mr Big' waved us a cheerful farewell.

'Did you see what he was reading?' asked Ann.

'No, I was dying to look,' I said. 'What was it?'

'*Othello*, in English,' she replied.

I decided I was going to like Mauritius very much.

CHAPTER TWO

PINK PIGEON PALAVER

The day on which we decided to go and hunt Pink pigeons dawned (if this is not too strong a word for such a dismal birth) and it appeared that the entire Indian Ocean from beginning to end was covered with a malevolent, swirling layer of thick cloud. In due course, this regurgitated floods of rain whose most noticeable attribute was that they were served at bath temperature. We gazed at the sky and cursed. This sort of weather was particularly annoying from two points of view.

Firstly, this was the only night in that week that we could receive the vital help of the Mauritian Special Mobile Force, the island's answer to the British Commandos and the American Marines, a stalwart body of men who, under their English Commanding Officer, Major Glazebrook, were to assist us in pigeon spotting and tree climbing, searchlight carrying and, eventually, we hoped, Pink pigeon capturing. Secondly, if this deluge of rain kept up, it would make any venture into the dripping and slippery forest futile in the extreme.

To our relief, mid-afternoon saw the break-up of the solid roof of cloud and blue patches started to appear like bits of a jigsaw on a dirty woollen shawl. By four o'clock, there was not a cloud in the sky and, in the warm air, the earth steamed gently. The blazing sun picked out all the raindrops trapped on the leaves and flowers so that they gleamed like some fallen galaxy of stars among the greens of the shrubs and trees. The Flamboyant trees that lined the road up towards the Pink pigeon forest had been battered by the fierce downpour and now each tree, aflame with scarlet and yellow blossom, stood in a great circle of mashed flowers as if rooted in a pool of its own blood.

In high spirits, we drove up the winding road towards the mountains. It was a road that curved and twisted as it climbed, now showing a wonderful vista of forest, its edges lapped by cane fields appearing as smooth and as bright as a billiard table from this height, and now and then showing us great shining sections of sea in halcyon array of blues with the reef, like a white garland of foam flowers, laid carelessly upon it. In the glittering bushes by the road, flocks of black and white bulbuls, with pointed crests and scarlet checks, fed among the leaves, sighing melodiously to each other; occasionally one would face another, raise its wings over its back like a tombstone angel, and flutter them gently in a delicate gesture of love. Sometimes, a mongoose would cross the road, slim, brindled, brisk, with a predatory Mafia gleam in its tiny eyes, nose to the ground as it snuffed its way to some blood-letting. We rounded one corner and came unexpectedly upon a troop of eight Macaque monkeys, sitting at the side of the road, their piggy eyes and air of untrustworthy arrogance making them look exactly like a board meeting of one of the less reliable consortiums in the City of London. The old male 'yaahed' out a staccato warning, the females gathered their megalocephalic Oliver Twist-thin babies to their breasts and the whole troop melted into the wall of Chinese guava that lined the road and disappeared with miraculous suddenness.

Eventually, we reached the Forestry Department's nursery of small trees and swung off the main highway on to a rough but serviceable track. Half a mile down this, and we saw Dave's car and the Army Land-Rover parked by the side of the track. Dave came bouncing over to greet us as we drew up.

'Hi,' he said, 'did you ever see such weather? Black as a mole's behind one minute, and blue as a monkey's backside the next. I really thought, with all that rain, we'd have to call the damn operation off. As it is, it'll be as wet as a well down there in the valley, but that's OK, we'll make out. Come and meet the guys.'

We decanted ourselves and our equipment from the car and followed him over to the Land-Rover. Standing by it, very smart in their green uniforms and berets, stood a group of soldiers, each as glossy as newly minted chocolate and of Herculean proportions. Their arms and legs were twice lifesize, their chests like firkins, their hands big enough to uproot whole trees, their smiles as wide and as glittering as any concert grand; yet, for all their Brobdingnagian proportions, they moved slowly and benignly, like Shire horses, beaming down at us lesser mortals from their exalted height. I decided, as they engulfed our puny hands in their gigantic, gentle paws, that I would rather have them on my side than against me. Their Commanding Officer, though not small by any standard, somehow looked slightly puny beside them.

Our military force had brought with them, as well as torches, nets and a portable searchlight, an enormous milk churn of tea, without which – as history relates – no British soldier or soldier trained by the British can possibly function smoothly and efficiently in outwitting and defeating the enemy. Making sure we all had our strange equipment, we set off in single file along a narrow path through the waist-high scrub, so laden with rain that we were soaked to the skin within a hundred yards.

Presently, the path dipped down into the valley and we were walking through a jungle of straight Chinese guava stems, interspersed here and there with a twisted, black ebony tree, or a group of Traveller's palms, like neat eighteenth-century fans whose handles had been stuck in the ground. The path was steep and knotted across it lay roots like varicose veins. The whole was drenched in rain so the water gleamed at every footstep in the mud, like a splintered mirror, and the mud itself turned into a caramel-coloured, sticky slide that, conspiring with the roots, could break a leg or an ankle as one would snap a stick of charcoal. The sun was starting to sink and shadows slanted across the path, which added further to the hazards. As we slid and tripped our way down into the valley, the air grew heavy and warm, and sweat was now added to make our condition even more aquatic. Presently we slid down a precipitous slope and the forest changed from a mixed assortment of plants to groves of cryptomeria trees, at first glance looking rather like a prickly species of pine tree, dark green with heavy bunches of needles.

'Pink Pigeon Valley,' said Dave, proudly. 'Took me an age to discover it. This is where most of them hang out.'

As he spoke, from the trees on our left came a loud, husky, seductive call: 'caroo, caroo, caroo, coo, coo, coo'.

There,' Dave exclaimed, 'there's one now. They've arrived early.'

With great enthusiasm, he threw back his head and imitated what appeared to be a whole flock of Pink pigeons in a variety of moods, ranging from anger to abject love. The real pigeons fell silent, seeming surprised by this sudden cacophony of sound, much as someone humming in the bath would be taken aback to be suddenly joined by the massed choirs of the Russian army.

'Funny,' said Dave, surprised. 'They generally answer. Oh well, we'd better spread out and start spotting, they'll all be coming in to roost pretty soon.'

Acting on his instructions, we spread out and made our way through the close-growing cryptomeria trees, seeking either trees we could climb and so view sections of the valley, or areas where there were breaks in the trees where we would get an uninterrupted sight of the pigeons flighting in. I found myself a large cryptomeria on a slope with branches growing practically down to the ground, so that scrambling up it was as easy as climbing a ladder. Some forty feet from the ground, I wedged myself into a convenient fork, unslung my binoculars and prepared to wait for the Pink pigeons. From my vantage point, I had a wide field of view which included a large slope of the cryptomeria forest where, Dave assured me, the pigeons roosted every night.

As I waited, I mused on the extraordinary method of capture that Dave had evolved. You arrived just before the sun went down and waited until the pigeons flighted in. When it was beginning to get dark they would flap heavily from wherever they were perching into another tree. This was the tree they would generally roost in, and it was this one that you had to mark. When it grew really dark, for the moon was fatal to such a venture, you approached the tree with torches, surrounded it and pinpointed the sleeping pigeon with your light beams. Then, quite simply, you shinned up the tree and either with your hands or a net shaped like a pair of sugar tongs, caught the bird, either soundly asleep still, or else awake but in a daze such as only a pigeon can get into. It sounded the most improbable technique but I had travelled in far too many countries and seen too many unlikely methods of capturing animals, to dismiss it out of hand.

The sun was now very low and the sky turned from a metallic kingfisher-blue to a paler, more powdery colour. The valley was washed with green and gold light, and the whole scene was calm and peaceful. A group of zosterops, minute, fragile, green birds, with pale, cream-coloured monocles round each eye, appeared suddenly in the branches above me, zinging and twittering to each other in high-pitched excitement as they performed strange acrobatics among the pine needles in search of minute insects. I pursed up my lips and made a high-pitched noise at them. The effect was ludicrous. They all stopped squeaking and searching for their supper, to congregate on a branch near me and regard me with wide eyes from behind their monocles. I made another noise. After a moment's stunned silence, they twittered agitatedly to each other and flapped inch by inch nearer and nearer to me until they were within touching distance. As long as I continued to make noises, they grew more and more alarmed and, with their heads on one side, drew closer and closer until they were hanging upside down a foot from my face, peering at me anxiously and discussing this strange phenomenon in their shrill little voices. I was just wondering whether I could get them actually to perch on me, when two Pink pigeons flew over the brow of the hill and settled in a cryptomeria fifty feet away. By raising my glasses to watch, I put my Lilliputian audience of zosterops to flight.

'Two have just flighted in,' shouted Dave from the stream bed at the bottom of the valley. 'Did anyone mark them?'

He had told me how tame the pigeons were, but I was still surprised to see these two billing and cooing in the tree, totally oblivious to Dave's shout.

'I've marked them,' I yelled back, and again was faintly astonished that the pigeons, who were very close to me, did not fly away, panic-stricken. They sat side by side on the branch, their breasts glowing pale cyclamen-pink in the rays of the sinking sun, occasionally rubbing beaks in what, for pigeons, was a passionate kiss. From time to time the one I took to be the male would bow to the female and give his loud, husky chant. The female, like all female pigeons, succeeded in looking vacant, affronted and hysterical all at once, like a Regency maiden about to have the vapours. Presently, the other pigeons flighted in and then there were four more; each one's arrival was greeted with a shout from one or other of our band. On one occasion, through my binoculars, I was watching Major Glazebrook climb laboriously to the straggling top branches of a cryptomeria on the other side of the valley, when a pair of pigeons flighted in and settled on a branch within six feet of him. Another one landed the same distance away from me and regarded me gravely for several minutes before deciding I might be dangerous and flying away. Given their tameness – or was it merely stupidity? – I was surprised that there were any of the species left, they presented such an easy target for an unscrupulous marksman.

We settled down, watching our respective pigeons, and as the sun sank, and the valley became washed in shadow, the birds flapped heavily from tree to tree. The pair I was watching flew languidly out of sight among the branches; I was just preparing to descend from my tree and go in search of them, when they reappeared and settled themselves comfortably on a high branch. They looked smug and satisfied, and I hoped that they had at last chosen their roost for the night, but just before it grew too dark to see them, to my intense annoyance, they took flight again. This time, fortunately, they only flew some twenty feet to a higher branch and there settled themselves. Gradually, the valley grew dark. I slowly eased my way down the tree to the ground – a not unhazardous undertaking. In the depths of the

valley, Dave, for some reason best known to himself, elected to impersonate an entire sounder of wild boar and was splashing about in the stream, grunting and squealing, screaming and moaning in the most lifelike fashion. It was calculated, one would have thought, to have given permanent insomnia to any Pink pigeons. However, it appeared to be a sound they were well used to and they slumbered on, uninterruptedly.

I made my way towards the tree in which my pigeons slept, plucking some fat, scarlet guavas en route to assuage my thirst. They were tart but pleasantly refreshing. Sitting with my back to the base of my pigeon tree, I ate a handful of them and my mouth felt less dry. Now that it was dark, the cicadas started, a shrill, whining zither that was ear-piercing. Not only did it seem to penetrate your skull like a trepanning job, but it had a ventriloquial effect, so that a cicada which appeared to be singing on your shoulder turned out to be thirty feet away. These insects were a little over an inch long, pale emerald-green with golden eyes, their shimmering wings looking like frosted-green church windows.

My head ringing with their exuberant cries, I gave my mind to the problem now on hand. Owing to the fact that we had to match our pigeon-catching exploits to the availability of our gargantuan Task Force, we had been forced to choose this evening, when the moon was half full, rather than an evening when there was no moon at all. This meant that now it was dark, we would have to move very fast and try to catch our birds before the moonlight became too strong and thus gave them sufficient light to escape by.

Presently, we were all congregated at the foot of my pigeon tree to discuss strategy. We decided that, as all the birds we had pinpointed – five in all – were widely scattered throughout the cryptomeria forest, we would start with the one in the smallest and most easily climbed tree nearest to the path and gradually work outwards to the others. Having decided this, we converged on the first tree and surrounded it with our torch beams and the blinding light of the portable searchlight, directed up into the branches where a fat, sleepy, bewildered pigeon sat some thirty-five feet above us.

At first sight, it looked extremely simple to shin up and grab or net the bird, but closer inspection revealed that the tree was so constructed that in order to climb it one would have to cause the maximum amount of noise and commotion. This could well startle the bird into launching itself into the frightening, black night. We had a rapid council of war in whispers, while the pigeon, now fully awake, watched us with benign interest. It was decided that the Sergeant, possibly the most gigantic of our force but the best tree climber, would scale one of the adjacent trees while John Hartley, who had long arms, would scale another. They would then endeavour to manoeuvre themselves into a position from which the capture of the pigeon would be possible. We decided not to plan any further at this stage since things tend to look different when you are dangling thirty-five feet up in the air.

The Sergeant started up his tree, massive but extraordinarily agile, and John Hartley, long-legged as a crane fly, started up his. The pigeon watched them coming aloft with deep interest untinged by alarm, its head slightly on one side. When the Sergeant and John had simultaneously reached a height equal to that of the pigeon's roost, they paused for breath, then in hoarse whispers confided to us that the Sergeant could edge along the branch to within netting distance of the bird. We eagerly told him to go ahead. We watched as he edged his twenty-odd stone of bone and muscle out along a branch that seemed too fragile to support a squirrel, let alone our ebony Goliath, but to our amazement he reached the end without it snapping.

Here, he manoeuvred the net into position. This net, as I have explained, was like a pair of sugar tongs with a net on each end. Clapped together, they caught the bird in the middle. At the sight of the net, the pigeon showed its first signs of wariness; that is to say, it put its head on one side and gave a slight flirt of its wings. The Sergeant now found that he needed to get another three feet closer to his prey and that this meant climbing to a higher branch. As the pigeon was now showing definite signs of unease, we decided to turn off our battery of lights and let the Sergeant get to his new vantage point in the dark as best he could. Some time, and a considerable amount of blasphemy later, he called down to us that he had successfully reached his new position.

We switched on our lights and discovered to our astonishment that the pigeon had seized this opportunity to tuck its head under its wing and snatch forty winks. When the lights came on again it pulled its head out from under its wing, with a gesture of irritability, and looked distinctly put out. The Sergeant, with an air of desperation, was now clinging to yet another fragile branch and working the net into position. Breathlessly, we watched him as he swept the net towards the pigeon; then we saw the bird, with surprising agility, hop farther down the branch but not fly away into the night. The Sergeant, clinging desperately to his bending, creaking branch, edged closer and took another swipe. This time, the two halves of the net snapped together and engulfed the bird, but the effort had been too much; Sergeant and branch bent downwards and in an effort not to let go and fall, he relinquished his hold on the handle of the net.

In silent horror, we watched it fall. The two sides of the 'sugar tongs' fell open so that our precious Pink pigeon was now only contained in one half of the net and could easily escape. Then

the falling net hit a tree limb and hung there. The pigeon gave a couple of half-hearted flaps and we waited to see if it would extricate itself from the net and fly away into the impenetrable gloom of the cryptomerias. However, after a token effort to escape, it lay stoically still, which was just as well as the net was only just hanging on to the branch.

Now we noticed something else. The branch in which the net was caught grew out at an angle and came quite close to the tree in which John Hartley was ensconced. Seeing this, John made his way rapidly down his tree and then out along the branches until he was separated from the net by a mere four-foot gap. With great care, since the branch he was on was both fragile and elastic, he reached across the gap. For a moment, I thought his arms were not long enough but then, to my relief, his hands closed round the mouth of the net. The Pink pigeon was ours.

Carefully, John eased his way back into the green depths of the cryptomeria where he transferred our capture from the net into one of the soft cloth bags with which he and the Sergeant had been provided. This safely done, he lowered the booty slowly down to the ground on a string. As the bag swung down out of the dark cryptomeria leaves, I received it reverently into my cupped hands. With great care, I opened it and extracted the pigeon for Dave to look at it. It lay quietly in my hands, without struggling, merely blinking its eyes in what appeared to be mild curiosity at this new experience. The colours seen so closely, even in an artificial light, were vivid and beautiful: the pale chocolates of the wings and the back, the rusty, almost fox-red of the tail and rump, and then the broad breast, neck and head, pale grey flushed with cyclamen-pink overtones. It was a remarkably handsome bird.

Gazing at it, feeling its silken feathering against my fingers and sensing the steady tremor of its heart-beat and its breathing, I was filled with a great sadness. This was one of the 33 individuals that survived; the shipwrecked remnants of their species, eking out a precarious existence on their cryptomeria raft. So, at one time, must a tiny group of Dodos, the last of their harmless, waddling kind, have faced the final onslaught of pigs, dogs, cats, monkeys and man, and disappeared for ever since there was no one to care and no one to offer them a breeding sanctuary, safe from their enemies. At least with our help, the Pink pigeons stood a better chance of survival, even though their numbers were down to such a dangerously low level.

We had taken so long over the capture of this pigeon that the moon had come out in strength and, to our annoyance, there was not a cloud in the sky. Any operation to capture more pigeons was doomed to failure, since there was more than enough light for them to see to fly by. Our first attempt to climb up to their roosts sent them flapping out of the cryptomeria branches and off down the valley. To try to track them down would have been a hopeless waste of time. As we tumbled and slipped and sweated our way out of the valley into a landscape brilliantly frosted by moonlight, we carried our precious burden, the Pink pigeon. We felt we could not complain. To have caught one bird out of the 33 in that sort of terrain and at the first attempt, struck me, in fact, as being little short of a miracle.

When we had got back to the hotel, showered, changed and anointed our mosquito bites, we assembled in the dining-room.

'Why don't we celebrate our capture,' I suggested. 'How about a dozen oysters and then some grilled lobster with green salad, followed by bananas flambéed in rum, washed down with a nice white wine?'

Both Ann and John said that, as a light snack, this met with their approval, and I gave the order accordingly. Presently, our waiter, who rejoiced in the name of Horace, came back.

'Please, Sir,' he said, 'I'm sorry for the lobsters.'

Although English is the official language of Mauritius, I had run into trouble from time to time. The Mauritian habit of saying 'mention' as an abbreviation for 'Don't mention it' when you thanked them, took a little getting used to. Now, I was faced with a new problem. Horace was sorry for the lobsters. Did this mean that, as a fully paid-up member of the RSPCA, the thought of the demise of these delectable crustaceans filled him with such remorse that he could not bring himself to serve them? Nothing in Horace's demeanour led me to believe this was so, but, at the same time, I did not want to risk hurting his feelings.

'Why are you sorry for the lobsters, Horace?' I asked, prepared to be gentle and sympathetic.

'Because there are no lobsters, Sir,' said Horace.

We had fish instead.

CHAPTER THREE

ROUND ISLAND

Unlike most sea expeditions undertaken in the tropics, our expedition to Round Island was an unqualified success; if, that is, you overlook the fact that Wahab was seasick, Dave suffered from heat-stroke, and I attempted to gain an Olympic Gold Medal for the longest most painful elbow-slide attempted to date on the island.

Getting up at four in the morning in a strange hotel is always sobering, especially when you suspect, from bitter experiences in other parts of the world, that you are the only member of the expedition who is being stupid enough to be on time, or, maybe, to appear at all. I always have a guilt complex when I get up too early in an hotel, and feel it incumbent upon me to creep about so as to avoid disturbing my less eccentric fellow guests. However, blundering about in unfamiliar territory is fraught with difficulties. On this occasion these started with trying to find the light switch, and knocking over the bedside table with its decoration of large water-jug, glass, clock, and three pamphlets on the fauna of Round Island. Next came the crashing descent of the lavatory seat (like a cannonade being fired across the bows of every sleeper in the place) to be followed by a rattle as of musketry as the waterpipes cleared their throats, merging into a roar of the shower which, at that hour, sounded like the cataclysmic eruption of Krakatoa in 1883. The only pleasure I derived from this whole dreary performance was the thought that I was waking my companions, who should have been up already.

Eventually, we piled sleepily into the car, complete with all the curious gear demanded of animal collectors (snake bags, nets, bottles, string, as well as cameras and binoculars), and drove off down the road, shiny wet with night rain between the whispering walls of sugar cane, towards the Yacht Club, at whose pier we were supposed to meet the rest of the party. Halfway there, luckily, we crossed paths with a car which contained Dave, who was driving in the wrong direction with great skill and confidence. Fortunately, he saw us, turned round and joined the cavalcade. Shortly afterwards, we came upon Wahab in his car, waiting under a tree to guide us; his wide, glittering, schoolboy grin was so mischievous and eager that we immediately felt not only confidence in the success of our mission, but even that getting up at four in the morning to accomplish it was a positive treat.

Arriving at the Yacht Club grounds, we parked our cars under the trees. Hopefully unseen by the Yacht Club's Garden Committee, John and I cut ourselves lengths of the bougainvillaea hedge to make lizard-catching sticks. Then, with our bags full of food and equipment, we trooped down the pier and surveyed our craft.

She was like a baby tug, with a tiny fore-deck, closed-in bridge-deck area, and a well-deck (with polished wooden benches around the perimeter) that was roofed, but otherwise open to whatever elements we were likely to encounter. She was snub-nosed and rather bossy-looking, with a practical ungainliness which somehow gave me confidence in her sea-going abilities. According to the brass plate fastened to her, she was nearly twenty years old, and had been built, of all unlikely places, in Colchester. She had started life with the somewhat butch name of *Corsair* but now had been re-christened the *Dorade*.

She already had a cargo of humanity aboard her for, apart from a very smart-looking captain in a peaked cap, there was his first officer, who looked like a young version of Haile Selassie; a tiny walnut of a man who was a diver (in case we sank, one supposed); a benign Moslem barrister, who was a friend of Wahab's; Tony Gardner and three forestry guards (who also 'belonged', so to speak, to Wahab); and a strange, portly gentleman, his sleepy-eyed, plump wife, and two female companions, all of them dressed in immaculate clothing which seemed more suitable for Henley regatta than the rigours of Round Island. As Wahab, Tony, and the rest of us joined them, I couldn't help reflecting that we looked not unlike the strangely ill-assorted collection of individuals that the Bellman had taken with him to hunt the Snark.

With a certain amount of shouting, argument, and rearrangement of people and belongings, as always happens on these occasions, we were safely settled in the well-deck area and our luggage bestowed. The ropes were cast off, and the good ship *Dorade* started on her way across a black, velvety sea, besprinkled with the waning star reflections, for the eastern sky was already pale with hosts of tiny, dark cumulus clouds like a flock of curly black sheep grazing on a silver meadow. The sea was incredibly calm and the wind warm and pleasant. Those of our number who had felt qualms about the sea-going ability of their internal organs relaxed perceptibly.

The first island we passed, looming large and dark on our left, was Gunner's Quoin, so-called because of its resemblance to the triangular-shaped piece of wood (like a flat-sided piece of cheese) that used to be wedged beneath a cannon to give it the right elevation and trajectory. Actually, as we chugged past it, I thought it looked more like the wreck of the *Titanic*, bottom-up and sinking by the stern. The dawn sky had now turned from silver to yellow. Those flocks of cumulus grazing on the horizon, became jet-black, with each curl rimmed in golden light, while the flocks that meandered higher in the pasture of the sky, turned slate blue with flecks and stripes of delicate purple. In the distance now, we could see the silhouette of Flat Island which, except for a protuberance at one end, lived up to its name. Then there was Ile aux Serpents, or Snake Island, like an inverted pudding basin, and lastly, our destination, Round Island, which, at that angle, did not look round at all but, with the aid of a certain amount of imagination, vaguely like a turtle with its head protruding from its shell, lying on the surface of the sea.

'Tell me,' I asked Tony, since geographical nomenclature, like the zoological, sometimes needs explanation, 'can you explain the anomaly of the names of those two islands?'

'Which ones?' asked Tony, puffing clouds of aromatic smoke from his pipe.

'Round Island and Ile aux Serpents,' I said.

'I don't quite see what you mean,' said Tony, puzzled.

'Well, Ile aux Serpents is round, and has no snakes inhabiting it, while Round Island is not round and is inhabited by two species of snake.'

'Ah, yes, that is curious,' admitted Tony. 'My own view is that they got the islands muddled up when they were drawing the maps. It can happen, you know.'

'I believe you,' I said. 'I once had an official map of the Cameroons which not only deflated a major town into a village, but shifted it two hundred miles north as well.'

Gradually, the whole sky lightened to powder-blue and shell-pink, and the clouds became smooth and white, piled up on the horizon like a snow-bedecked group of trees. Then, suddenly, through this forest of cumulus, the sun shouldered its way like a tiger, and burnt a glittering path of light across the sea, that seemed to catch the *Dorade* in claws of heat, even at that early hour.

The closer we got to Round Island, the more forbidding did the terrain appear. The sun was rising almost directly behind it, so that we saw it mainly in silhouette, rising, apparently sheer from the sea, with a tattered fringe of palms along part of its summit. The good ship *Dorade* shouldered its way across a blue swell that was, though not fierce, languidly muscular, and gave the impression of great power, like a half-asleep blue cat.

'I'm glad it's so calm,' said Tony. 'In fact, it's the calmest I've ever seen it. Sometimes, it takes over an hour to land, and they frequently have to cut the anchor adrift if it catches under one of the submarine ledges.'

'I know,' I said. 'I read with reverence, not unmixed with awe, Nicolas Pike's description of his sojourn on Round Island. His account of his first landing gives one pause for thought.'

'Yes. Remarkable man,' said Tony.

Pike was one of those indefatigable Victorian explorers, to whom present-day naturalists and zoologists owe such a great debt as, in their extraordinary unsuitable clothing but with bright, alert, all-embracing minds, they circumnavigated the world, cataloguing everything they saw, recording everything they heard, insatiable in their thirst for knowledge, and most of them, blessed with a strange, archaic style of writing and a sense of humour of the variety generally only found in the more ancient volumes of *Punch*. Their accounts of what they saw and collected have a freshness, enthusiasm and appeal which is generally lacking in the flaccid travel books foisted on us nowadays by the naturalist traveller of the jet set. Here, for example, was Nicolas Pike setting foot on Round Island for the first time:

I at once saw that what had been told me of the difficulty of landing was no exaggeration. Luckily, our fishermen crew made their arrangements skilfully. The boat was allowed to drift within a few feet of the table rock, our landing place, against which the waves were breaking.

At this stage we had to wait, and watch for an opportunity for one of our crew to jump ashore with a rope, so that the boat might be kept bow on and steady. When this was effected, the rope was securely fastened to iron rings placed there for that purpose years ago; and then our provisions, water, etc., were passed on shore.

When everything was safely landed, each one watched for the moment when the boat rose, and sprung on to the rock with a bound that made every nerve quiver; and it needed a sure foot and steady eye to alight firmly on the slippery stone.

If our little craft, which rose and fell some ten or twelve feet, had struck her bows on the precipitous ledge, she would have been hurled to Davy Jones's Locker, and all in her, in a few seconds. The depth of the water is about four fathoms here.

As the *Dorade* rose and sank on the polished blue rollers, I could see what Pike meant. Scanning the cliffs we were now approaching, I could not spot a single place suitable for setting ashore anything less agile than a mountain goat.

'Where is the landing area?' I enquired of Tony.

'There,' he said, gesturing vaguely towards the apparently perpendicular rock face. 'That flat area of rock; that's where Pike landed.'

Peering closely, I could just make out a flat protuberance of rock that looked about the size of a dining-room table, against which the blue sea shouldered in a suggestive manner.

'There?' I asked, disbelievingly.

'There,' said Tony.

'I don't wish to seem over-critical,' I said, 'but it looks to me as though one would have to be a cross between an exceptionally agile gecko and a Sherpa to get on to that.'

'Don't worry, Gerry,' said Wahab, grinning, 'you can only die once.'

'I know,' I said. 'That's why I'm so anxious not to squander the experience by using it up too soon.'

'Calmest day I've ever seen. There'll be no difficulty,' said Tony, seriously.

There was great activity up in the bows and the anchor rattled overboard into about forty feet of gin-clear water.

'That's the cave that Nicolas Pike sheltered in when he was caught in the cyclone,' said Wahab, pointing at the half-moon scoop out of the rocks alongside the landing site.

'The roof's fallen now, but you can still see the shape of it,' added Tony.

I gazed at the half-circle carved out of the cliff bedecked now with a host of shiny, black mud-skippers (that crawled in a most un-fish-like way over the rocks) and a bevy of scarlet and purple crabs, and I remembered Pike's hair-raising description. It was the actual place, I realised with a feeling of reverence, where he almost lost his 'unwhisperables':

Busy as we were, the elements were collecting their forces more energetically still; and at half-past six the sea suddenly began to roll in heavily, and very soon volumes of water, ten or twelve feet deep, poured over the table rock, where our party had embarked only two hours previously. The wash of the waves swept off our water casks that were about fifty yards from it, and at an elevation of about twenty-five feet; and they were not long before they surged into the cave, nearly reaching the spot where we stood watching the scene in dismay, and cutting off our retreat.

The captain of the boat, as soon as he saw the sudden change in the weather, raised his anchor and scudded off before the wind, and we soon lost sight of him in the heavy rolling billows.

All efforts now were turned to securing everything as far as was practicable; but the night was well set in before we had finished, and the whole sky was overcast with heavy clouds. The reverberations of the deep rolling thunder made the mountain tremble, and the vivid flashes of lightning occasionally lit up the foaming, seething mass of waters below us, madly dashing against the rocks, the spray thoroughly drenching us.

Then came the rain in a deluge to add to our troubles; and it was not long before the torrents rushing down the mountain poured over the precipice forming the roof of our cave, in a cascade twenty feet wide, bringing with them stones of all sizes, that struck the bottom of the cave with great force, and then bounded off into the sea, now and then giving us a sharp blow. Here we remained, the sea gradually encroaching on our quarters, till we were obliged to crowd in the farthest comers, and hold on to prevent our being washed away. Matters were getting too exciting to be pleasant, and we felt some effort must be made to escape from our perilous position.

The day before, a long rope had been strongly attached to the rock above and one end was hanging down over the precipice; but unluckily it had been placed on the lowest part, where the heaviest body of water was falling. Fortunately, the rope was long, and my comrade emerged from his hiding-place, and, watching his chance, seized the rope and, holding on like grim death, managed to draw it in, and worked it along away from the cascade, thus succeeding in hitching it over the projecting side of the rock, which showed a perpendicular face about thirty feet high. I never saw anything more bravely done, and at the risk of his life, for, a false step, and nothing could have saved him; as it was, he got a severe contusion on his head and side from a stone striking him.

Nothing daunted, the plucky little fellow, as the smallest and lightest man amongst us, was the first to ascend the rope; and I confess the time we were waiting for the welcome signal of his safe arrival was one of awful suspense, for it was a mere chance if the rope held out, or if he could fight against the wind and driving rain.

At last, to our great joy, above the roar of the elements we heard his welcome 'all right!' I next ascended, and, divested of all but an old blue shirt and trousers, I grasped the rope and swung on to the projecting cliff, and commenced mounting, hand over hand. It was nervous work, swinging thus in mid air, between life and death, as a slip would have sent me into the yawning gulf below. I was soon high enough to rest my feet on the side of the rock, and could hear my friend urging me on in a voice that seemed to come from the clouds. I felt desperately thankful when I arrived at the top, in spite of my hands and feet being lacerated and bleeding, and my body bruised all over, to say nothing of the loss of the greater part of my unwhisperables.

Our landing on Round Island was considerably less hair-raising than Pike's experience had been. No sooner had the anchor got a grip on the ocean bed than Tony and the diver slid overboard like otters, carrying two ropes, and soon these were made fast from the *Dorade* to the shore. As a spider lets forth a thread of silk, waits for it to catch, and then uses it as a guide-line, so these two ropes were to be our guide-lines along which we were to pull and steer the dinghy to the landing site. So we loaded our baskets of food and equipment into the dinghy, piled in ourselves, and were pulled shorewards.

Now we were closer, with the glare of the sun hidden behind the bulk of the island, we could see for the first time what a curious geological formation it was. The whole island was composed of tuff, and this soft stuff had been smoothed and sculpted by the wind and rain into pleats and scallops, so that the whole island was like a gigantic stone crinoline dropped on the surface of the sea, with here and there, standing up like jagged brocade, turrets, arches, and flying buttresses carved by the elements. I was sorry to see that the only part of the island that appeared to be remotely flat was the rocky area that formed the landing stage. The rest rose precipitously in what appeared to be an unclimbable rock face.

There was no time to worry about what awaited us on the island, for the tricky moment of disembarkation had arrived. It bore no resemblance to the difficulties that Pike had encountered at this very same spot, but even though it was the calmest anyone could remember, the boat was still lifted and lowered some three feet by the swell, and the bows of the dinghy scrunched and splintered when they touched the rock. The landing was no more difficult than stepping off the back of a rocking-horse on to a nursery table, but the way even that apparently gentle swell could grind the dinghy against the rocks, made you fully aware of the bone-crushing results if you were to miss your footing and place a leg between the boat and the shore. However, both we and the gear were landed without mishap. Picking up our various baskets and bags, we followed Wahab and Tony up the slope between the strangely sculptured pinnacles of rock.

'Will you get these rocks?' panted Dave. 'Aren't they the damnedest thing you've ever seen? A sort of Round Island Grand Canyon.'

A White-tailed tropic bird hung in the sky above us like an ivory Maltese Cross, screaming peevishly, and Dave paused to wipe the sweat from his eyes and reply to it with what appeared to be a blast of invective in its own tongue. Startled, the bird slid away on the wind and disappeared.

'Aren't they the most beautiful God-damned birds you've ever seen?' enquired Dave.

I made no reply. Weighted down with a 'fridge-full of iced drinks and a selection of cameras and binoculars, I had

no breath for imitations or speech, and I wondered how
Dave had. The surface of the rock appeared smooth, but in
places it was covered with a thin crust, ready to peel away,
like the skin off an over-enthusiastic sunbather's back,
and in other parts with a fine smattering of granules. Both
these surfaces, if trodden on unwarily, made one's feet
slide, which either meant that one lost a yard of ground
or that one slid ungracefully, and with ever increasing
momentum, into the sea below. Although it was only seven
o'clock, the air was warm and moist and sticky with salt,
and the sweat poured down us in torrents. The equipment
became heavier with each step and the slope appeared to
become more vertical as we climbed. Wahab paused above
us and looked back, grinning and wiping the sweat from
his bronze face.

'It is not far now,' he called. 'There is the picnic tree.'

I looked to where he was pointing, and there, high above us
(as unattainable as the tip of Everest), I saw the curious fan-
like leaves of the pandanus, beckoning us like green hands.
It seemed an age before we reached the tree, which stood on
a series of thick, leg-like roots. We paused thankfully in the
small pools of shade cast by its leaves, stacked the food in
the shade and sorted out the equipment we needed for our
hunt. As we did this, there suddenly emerged from every
nook and cranny around us, as if summoned by the flute of
some invisible Pied Piper, a host of large, fat, shiny skinks
with bright, intelligent eyes.

'Look!' croaked John, his spectacles misting over with
emotion. 'Just look at them! Telfarii.'

'Yes, yes,' said Wahab, beaming at John's obvious delight.
'They are very tame. They always join the picnic under the
tree. Later, we will feed them.'

'Did you ever see anything so God-damned cute?' demanded Dave. 'Just look at those sons-of-bitches. Tame as a chorus of rabbits.'

The skinks were handsome lizards with heavy, square-looking bodies, short legs, and long tails. They held their heads high as they moved with graceful, slithering motions towards us and proceeded to climb all over our piles of equipment. They were coloured a sober but pleasing shade of grey or brown, but when the sunlight hit them at a certain angle, their smooth scales, like mosaic-work, suddenly bloomed into purple, green, peacock-blue and gold, rainbowed like a film of oil on a roadside puddle. This skink, Telfair's skink or telfarii, was one of the species we had come so far to collect, and far from appearing elusive, here was a welcoming committee going through our baggage with all the thoroughness of a band of elegant Customs officers.

Since these specimens seemed so eager to be caught, it seemed to us more sensible to concentrate on the two other species we had come for. One was Gunther's gecko, of which it had been estimated that only five hundred specimens remained on the island, and the other a small species of skink which, Tony and Wahab informed us encouragingly, only inhabited the summit of Round Island. Tony suggested that it would be a good idea to search for the Gunther's gecko first, since they inhabited scattered palm trees on the western slopes of the island, which would not, as yet, have received the full force of the sun.

Before we set out, Wahab, with a great flourish, produced a bag of straw hats he had chosen for everyone. The majority were broad-brimmed and these he reserved for us, as guests. In consequence, the only one he could find for himself was a cloche hat belonging to his wife, in elegant magenta and white straw, with a pink ribbon to tie under the chin. This, he donned with perfect seriousness, and was somewhat surprised at our laughter.

'But the sun is very hot,' he explained, 'and one needs a hat.'

'And very beautiful you look, Wahab,' said Ann. 'Don't take any notice of them. They're only jealous because they don't look so handsome.'

Thus placated, Wahab gave us his searchlight grin and insisted on wearing his ridiculous headgear for the rest of the day.

We had landed some three-quarters of the way down the eastern side of the island, and we now made our way along the slopes towards the northern tip, moving among the scattered Round Island palms and the thickets of pandanus which grew in patches on the barren hillside. As well as being moulded into smooth longitudinal folds and ridges, the soft tuff had been gouged out in places by winter rains and the last cyclone (delicately, and inappropriately, called 'Gervaise') into long, deep gashes in the hillside, running from the steep upper slopes down to the sea, down which were carried avalanches of what top-soil remained and rocks of considerable size. Some of these ravines were, in places, ten to fifteen feet in depth, and forty to fifty feet across. I thought bitterly, as I panted my way moistly across the scorching rocks, that this moonscape had been created by the interference of man.

We had hardly travelled a hundred yards, spread out, and peering hopefully at every palm frond, when Wahab sang out that he had found a guntheri. We scrambled and panted our way across the hot rocks, tripping over the small weed, not unlike a convolvulus, which in places formed mats covered with pale lavender and pink flowers and was, in spite of the rabbits, making a valiant but forlorn attempt to keep the soil in position against the onslaught of rain and wind. When we reached Wahab, he pointed up at the main stem of a pandanus frond. Having wiped the sweat from my eyes, I peered up, and eventually saw the guntheri, spread-eagled and flattened, with its mottled-grey and chocolate skin, lichen-grey flecked, making it look like a discolouration on the bark. It was large for a gecko, being some eight inches long, with great, golden eyes and plate-like protuberances on its toes, which contain the suction pads which enable it to hang on to the smooth surface with a fly-like ability. It clung there, secure in the feeling that it was well enough camouflaged, regarding us calmly from great, golden brown-flecked eyes with vertical pupils, which gave it a strange cat-like appearance.

'Will you look at that?' panted Dave. 'Isn't that the largest God-damned gecko you've ever seen? What a magnificent specimen!'

After some argument, we decided that the honour of the first capture belonged to Dave. He prepared himself on a safe foothold, and then edged the bamboo pole forward, the

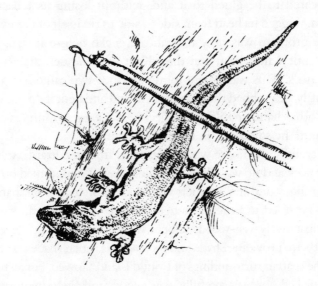

nylon noose dangling from the end, flittering like a fish scale in the sunlight. I prayed that this sparkle would not panic the lizard, but he hung there without movement, regarding us benevolently. We all held our breath, while Dave moved the noose forward inch by inch. Now he had it dangling just in front of the gecko's nose. This was the crucial moment, for he had to ease the noose over the animal's head and then snap it tight round its fat neck, all without alarming it. Slowly, by infinitesimal stages, he stroked the nylon down the palm rib. Just when it was almost touching the gecko's nose, the animal raised its head and looked with interest at the noose. We all froze. Several seconds passed, and then, as gently as though he were stroking a spider's web, Dave eased the noose, millimetre by microscopic millimetre, over the creature's head. Then he took a deep breath and jerked the noose tight round the gecko's neck. The gecko tightened his grip on the branch, so that it appeared to be glued to it and, without losing its tenacious hold, wagged its head from side to side to rid itself of the nylon. The problem was now to grab the gecko before it struggled too much and the nylon thread cut into the delicate skin of the neck. This was where John's six-foot-two came in useful. Swiftly, he grabbed the base of the frond and bent it down, with the other hand engulfing the gecko, as it came within reach. 'Got it!' he squeaked, in tremulous triumph.

Carefully, the noose was disentangled from the lizard's velvety soft neck and he was placed in a cloth bag. We continued on our way, and found the guntheri was much more common than we had been led to believe, though this side of the island, with its comparatively well-wooded slopes, was obviously a favourite resort for them, providing shade and food – or as much shade and food as the spartan surroundings of Round Island allowed. For an hour, we picked our way carefully over ravines and along the tortured slopes, where an incautious foot would send rocks bounding and crashing down the precipitous slopes, carrying avalanches of dry tuff with them. Frequently, multicoloured rabbits scurried out from under our feet, and we came upon numerous signs of their profligate tenancy: the convolvulus-type creeper cropped; low, baby palms with their tops amputated; slopes burrowed into so as to cause the maximum erosion.

We had walked about a quarter of the circumference of the island. The sun, which when we had started had been hidden behind the bulk of the island, now rose above it. It was like standing in front of a suddenly open oven door. The air seemed thick to breathe, almost like a soup of moisture, heavily larded with salt. The Martian landscape shimmered in the heat haze as though it was under water.

It was interesting to watch my companions. Ann had wandered off somewhere by herself, and so we were an all-male group.

Wahab, wearing his ridiculous poke-bonnet, was peering up into the palms earnestly, humming to himself and periodically producing from his pocket a paper bag, full of sticky sweets, and offering them round. John, tall and lanky, glasses always on the point of misting over completely, was quivering with eagerness, determined not to waste a single instant of this time in the herpetological paradise that he had dreamt and talked of for so long. Then there was Dave, with his trumpet voice, anxious and enthusiastic, as full of snap, crackle and pop as any breakfast cereal, spilling superlatives out like a Hollywood film advertisement, interspersed with more animal noises than are necessary for the successful rendering of 'Old MacDonald Had a Farm'. Then Tony, dressed in his faded green shirt and khaki trousers, merging into the landscape like a chameleon, answering any query with a staccato flood of information, by far the most un-fussed and organised of us all. From a minute basket, he seemed able to produce at any given moment anything from hot tea to marmalade sandwiches, from cold curry and rice to orange squash. So impressed was I by this conjurer's ability that I felt, if asked, Tony could have produced a dining-table, candelabra, napery, dinner jackets, so that we could have sat down on the bleak slopes of Round Island, and partaken of a meal in the traditional way that, mythology assures us, Englishmen observe in the tropics.

Within a couple of hours, we had caught all the guntheri that we were permitted to catch, and so, we sat and roasted in a minute carpet of shade provided by a group of palmettos. John managed to find sixteen new joints in his body and to curl up in an area that would have been cramped for a chihuahua. Wahab wound himself round the palm tree and distributed glutinous sweets of thirst-provoking quality. Tony squatted on his haunches against a convolvulus-covered rock and vanished completely against the background, to reappear unnervingly at intervals, like the Cheshire Cat, to offer us orangeade or a marmalade sandwich. Dave sprawled between three patches of leaf shade the size of soup plates, and carried on a long and acrimonious exchange with the tropic birds that, with their long, needle-like tails and pointed wings and beaks, wheeled and dived above us like some constellation of mad shooting stars, uttering their shrill, whining cries. Wahab showed us that, by waving something white, a handkerchief, a snake bag or a shirt, you could get them to dive low at you. This excitement, combined with the endless cacophony of repartee that Dave indulged in, soon had some twenty or thirty birds around us, wheeling, diving and calling, white as sea foam against blue sky.

'Now,' said John, starting to quiver with eagerness again after our brief rest, 'what do we do now?'

'Well,' said Tony, re-emerging from his background, 'if you want to... you know, want to catch some of the smaller... the smaller skinks, they tend to live on top of the island, so we'd better go straight up to the top.'

He jerked his thumb behind us. I thought he was joking. The slope we had been walking along was so steep that it made you feel that you would have been happier if one of your legs had been three foot longer than the other, but behind us rose something as sheer, as unfriendly, and as dangerous-looking as the Jungfrau in a heat wave, devoid alike, as far as one could see, of both foot and hand-holds.

'I was growing to like you, Tony, 'I said, 'but you really must try to curb this macabre sense of humour you display. If anyone took you seriously, someone of my noble proportions and youthfulness, for example, he might easily suffer a cardiac arrest by dwelling on your facetious remark.'

'I'm not joking,' said Tony. 'It's the best way up, and it's quite easy if you zig-zag.'

'Zig-zag,' said Dave. 'What sort of a God-damned nonsense is that? You'd have to be a mountain goat with adhesive feet to zig-zag up that.'

'I assure you, it's not nearly as bad as it looks,' said Tony, firmly.

'We forgot the oxygen mask,' said Wahab, 'so if we hold our breath until the top, it will help.'

'I cannot think why I associate with you all,' I said. 'And I can't think why I was stupid enough to come to this place in the first place.'

'You wouldn't have missed *this*, would you?' asked John, incredulously, as if I had uttered a blasphemy.

'No,' I admitted, as I got to my feet and picked up my camera. 'I probably wouldn't. They say there's no fool like an old fool.'

We started tacking up the precipitous slope. Reluctant though we were to admit it, we found that Tony was right, and that which had seemed unclimbable, when viewed from below, became more or less possible if we zig-zagged like a drunken centipede. Here and there, we were startled by loud, belligerent, witch-like screams, apparently issuing from the bowels of the earth. These proved to be caused by Red-tailed tropic birds, sitting in their nesting cavities under the slabs of lava, endeavouring to frighten us away. They were the size of small gulls, with tern-like heads, large, melting eyes and sealing-wax-red beaks. The plumage on the head, breast and wing butts was a delicate, glittering, pale rose-pink, as if they had been bathed in some vat of ethereal dye. When their maniacal screams proved to be unsuccessful in frightening us off, they just sat there and stared at us. It is this stupid habit of sitting still and accepting their fate that is the chief reason for their slaughter, for they are an easy prey for the fishermen who land on Round Island to kill them and take their bodies back to Mauritius, where they are sold to the Chinese restaurants.

The summit seemed unreachable. Every time we breasted a slope, thinking it was the top, another wall of rock faced us. At last we really did arrive at a completely flat area covered with slabs of rock, lying scattered about as if dropped haphazardly from the skies. It was a much hotter terrain than the cliff-sides, since nothing but sparse mats of convolvulus grew between the rocks, and not even the most spindly of pandanus provided shade. Here there were no guntheri, but instead small skinks, some four-and-a-half inches in length, with a long tail and pointed head, and such small legs they looked almost snake-like. They slithered like drops of quick-silver, their movements baffling the eye, as quick as a humming-bird's.

'Well, will you look at these? Will you just look at these?' panted Dave. 'Aren't these the smallest God-damned things you've ever seen? Aren't they the cutest little fellas?'

The skinks, bright-eyed, fluid and quick as raindrops on a window, continued their never-ending movement, oblivious of the lavish praise that was being bestowed upon them. Their smooth, shiny scales, pale-green and coffee-coloured, shone in the sunshine, and they did not deviate from the stern task of food hunting, except to hurl themselves at each other in mock combat, should their paths cross. Dave wiped his hands on his trousers, took a firm grip on the lizard stick, and approached a rather large and well-built skink which was going through the crevices of a rock with all the thoroughness of a Scotland Yard detective searching a tenement building for drug smugglers. His efficiency and dedication to duty would have won him a recommendation from any Chief of Police. He took no notice whatsoever as Dave loomed over him.

'Come along, then, little fella,' crooned Dave, noose dangling expectantly. 'Come on, then.'

He dangled the noose in front of the lizard and the glitter of the nylon caught its eye. It paused and raised its head and Dave deftly slipped the noose round its neck, pulled it tight, and lifted. You might as well have tried to catch a rainbow. The smooth scales formed a polished surface for the nylon to slide on, and the weight of the lizard's body slid its head out of the noose with no difficulty. The lizard, which had been lifted and then dropped some six inches, was completely unperturbed by his brief flight. He paused to lick his lips thoroughly and then proceeded on his insect hunting as if nothing had happened. Twice more, Dave got the noose over his head and twice more it slipped off, as if the skink had been buttered.

'God damn it, the little bastards are as slippery as a barrel of lard,' said Dave, mopping his face. 'Did you ever see anything so damned agile? And the little bastard's not scared, either. Are you, you son of a gun? Now, are you going to let Dave catch you, or aren't you, little fella?'

Thus adjured, the lizard paused, licked his lips, yawned in Dave's face and continued on his quick, excited hunt for six-legged comestibles. Four more times, Dave attempted to catch the skink, and four more times he failed. The amusing thing was that the skink seemed totally oblivious to the fact that he kept making short journeys into space; whenever he slid out of the noose and landed with a thump, he resumed his hunting, unflurried and with unabated enthusiasm.

In the end, since it was obvious that the noose would not work on such an apparently liquid species, John caught him by hand. We unanimously agreed that this was the best (if the most exhausting) way of doing it. We'd been employing this method for some time, when I became aware of an almost total lack of shade on the summit. There were no trees, and the only shadows were cast by the tumbled landscape of rocks, but now it was getting on for midday, and the sun was almost vertical above us, so that the shade the rocks were producing was negligible. I became worried about our bags, full of precious guntheri; so it was decided that I would leave the others hunting, and make my way back to the picnic tree, which would provide enough shade for our precious specimens. So I departed, carrying the bundle of cloth bags in the shade of my body, leaving the others quartering the hot, dry terrain like hounds, shouting to each other: 'Look out! He's going under there.' 'Quick! Quick! Get on the other side as he comes out,' and: 'Hell! I can't turn the bloody rock over.'

Slowly, picking my way among the tumbled boulders, I made my way along the spine of the island until I felt that I was more or less opposite the picnic tree site. Then, I approached the precipitous slope and looked for the *Dorade* as a landmark. While we'd been stupid enough to leave the safety of the boat and blunder about in the sun after a load of lizards, the Henley regatta crowd had done no such thing; they had paid a visit to a reef some half a mile away to indulge in cool underwater swimming and fishing. As I looked down the hillside to the sea, I could see the *Dorade*, white and trim, looking about the size of a matchbox, steaming towards the landing spot. I made my way a short distance down the slope and found a young palm tree that was giving something approximating to shade. There I squatted, sheltering my precious cargo, watching the *Dorade* and waiting for her to anchor, so that I could get my bearings. From the top of the island, the whole terrain looked completely different, and I could not see the picnic tree at all. As I had no desire to walk farther than was necessary in that blistering heat, I thought that I would wait for the *Dorade* to act as a marker. Presently she chugged from the royal blue and purple deep sea into the jay's-wing blue and jade-green of the shallow water, and dimly I heard her anchor rattle overboard. I mopped my face, hoisted my camera on to my shoulder, picked up my bags of geckos and started down towards the sea.

I very soon discovered that to attain my objective was as difficult as Alice had found making progress in the Looking-Glass garden. Normally, if you have a high vantage point, you can more easily pinpoint your goal than if you are on a level with it, but in the case of Round Island things were different. As I have said, the island is like a stone crinoline dropped on the seas surface, and whichever pleat you happen to be standing on, it is almost impossible to see the rest of the garment. After I had lost the boat twice, and had had to turn back or aside three times because I had reached such sheer sheets of rock that it seemed imprudent to go on, unless I was seeking a broken leg, I suddenly spotted, far below me a flash of scarlet. This, I knew, was a towel I had brought and had draped over the spare film and various foods under the picnic tree to provide some sort of shade.

This, then, was going to act as my marker.

I clattered and slid on my way, keeping the little red splash firmly in sight. I rested for a second time under a small group of pandanus, whose tattered leaves drummed against each other nervously and whispered sibilantly in a sudden puff of hot wind from the sea. Carefully, I felt my geckos in their bags to make sure they were not being affected by their journey. The sharp nip which one of them administered led me to believe that they were faring a good deal better than I was. I had sweated so profusely that I felt that if I lost another cupful of moisture, I would turn into a ginger-bread crumble and blow away. It was only the thought of the iced drinks that awaited me under the picnic tree that kept me going.

Grimly, I shouldered my load and plodded on. I came presently to a great, almost sheer precipice of rock, the top half of which was decorated by a tiny mat of convolvulus-like weed, starred with pale pink flowers. To reach a ravine that led down towards a lower level, I had to cross this dangerous bit of rock, and so decided, in case the exposed portion was slippery, that I would walk on the carpet of weed. Slowly, I edged my way across, making sure of one step before I took another. I was just congratulating myself on my climbing skill, when I inserted one foot into a natural noose formed by the creeper, tripped, and fell heavily on to my back My camera went skittering off joyfully, and I held my bag of lizards aloft, so that at least I wouldn't fall on them.

I'd landed on my spine with such force that I heard what appeared to be my whole vertebral column play a rapid tune, producing the sort of noise that is usually only obtained by the use of maracas. I had landed on the bare rock and as there was nothing I could grab hold of to prevent my sliding, I proceeded down the rock face on my back with ever-increasing speed, gathering around me an avalanche of loose tuff and bits of extremely sharp lava. As my momentum increased, my body started to turn so that presently I knew I should be on my stomach. I was terrified lest I should twist and inadvertently roll on to my bag of lizards, which I still held in a tenacious grip. I didn't dare let go of them, for if they had lodged on that inhospitable sheet of rock it was probable that I would not be able to climb up to retrieve them.

There was only one thing to be done, and that was to use my elbows as a brake. This I did, and was gratified to discover that the pain I suffered was not in vain. Not only did I remain on my back and my shredded elbows but I slowed down my pace of descent, and eventually actually stopped. I lay still for a moment to savour my wounds to the full, and then moved bits of my body experimentally to see if anything was broken. To my surprise, nothing was, and the amount of gore my right arm was producing was out of all proportion to the wounds it had sustained. Painfully, I shuffled sideways across the rock face, retrieved my camera, which was intact, and gained the ravine where the going was easier. At the first group of palms I came to, I sat down, made sure my geckos and my camera had sustained no injuries, and mopped up the blood from my elbows. Then after a brief pause, I got to my feet and gazed down towards my red landmark, by the sea.

It had completely disappeared.

Not only had it disappeared, but the *Dorade* had disappeared as well, and the view now lying below me bore no resemblance to any terrain I had seen or walked through that day. To say that I was irritated by these circumstances, is putting it mildly; I was hot, exhausted, thirsty and aching all over, and I had a severe headache. For all the indications to the contrary, I might have been in the middle of Australia, fifty miles north of Lhasa, or on one of the more inimical craters of the moon. Making a blasphemous commentary on my own stupidity in falling I set off down the ravine in what I hoped was the right direction. It seemed to be an area singularly lacking in palms, and eventually I was forced to crouch and rest in a tiny patch of shade caused by a hummock in the sides of the ravine. Grimly, I plodded on and soon, to my delight, could hear voices and various nautical noises that told me I was near the landing stage. How close, I did not realise until I rounded I dump of rock and found myself practically on the shore. High above me was the picnic tree and my red towel. I had somehow misjudged my descent, with the result that some two hundred and fifty feet above me lay shade, cool drinks and salve for my various contusions.

The last climb was the worst. The blood pounded in my ears my head ached, and I was forced to rest frequently. Finally I staggered up the last slope and collapsed in the fretted shade of the picnic tree. A few minutes after, Dave arrived, looking, I was delighted to see, as fragile as I felt. When I could speak, I asked him how he had fared, and he confessed that he had passed out a couple of times with the heat. He certainly looked white and ill-kempt. Soon he was regaling me with an account of his adventures. The worst moment had been when John Hartley, coming upon the recumbent Dave, had made an effort to rally him but had got sidetracked when he spied a large telfairii and various geckos sitting close together. Having captured these and finding nothing more suitable to put them in, he promptly and callously commandeered Dave's tee shirt and handkerchief and continued on his way triumphant, leaving Dave to make out as best he could. This made John one of the people least likely to succeed in a Good Samaritan contest, according to Dave.

'Just left me there,' Dave confided to me, croakingly. 'Just high-tailed off and left me useless as the tits on a boar hog and twice as undecorative. That John's inhuman, I'm telling you. Can you understand a guy who'd let a fella human die for the sake of a gecko, for God's sake?'

He was still busy embroidering his experience, complete with death-rattle, bird calls, and the jeering cries of callous lizards, when the others straggled back to the picnic tree. They were all in various stages of exhaustion, with the exception of Tony who looked, if anything, slightly cooler and more immaculate than when he had set out. The others dived for the shade and the cool drinks, whereas Tony squatted in the full glare of the sun and, with a few magic passes, conjured out of thin air a cup of steaming tea and some glutinous, but doubtless nourishing, chutney sandwiches.

After we had revived somewhat, we set about the last task; to catch some of the Telfair skinks which surrounded us in such profusion that one had to be careful where one sat, and where one placed one's cup or food. A peanut-butter sandwich that Dave misguidedly placed on the rock by his side while he drank, was seized and disputed by two large Telfair skinks before he could rescue it, and disappeared down the hill in a sort of whirling rugger-scrum. Another large Telfair seized on a banana skin and, with his head held high, rushed off over the rocks like a standard bearer, with a host of eager skinks tearing after him. He reached a group of palmettos some distance away without having to relinquish his trophy, but the ownership of it was still being disputed vigorously when we left the island half an hour later.

With the skinks behaving like domestic animals, it was no trouble at all just to sit there, choose one's specimen and simply drop the noose over its head as it investigated a Thermos flask, a sandwich, or a Coca-Cola bottle. Occasionally, there were so many around us at one time that we would make a mistake and catch the wrong one (a male instead of a female, say). The animal would then be released, and having indignantly given us a swift and painful bite, would continue its examination of our belongings as if nothing had happened.

At last, we had our quota of these enchanting tame lizards and packed up to leave Round Island. We were aching, tired, and sun-blistered, but we wouldn't have missed the experience for anything. We had not seen either of the two species of snake (which was not surprising, considering their limited numbers) and we had not captured the strictly nocturnal gecko, but our collecting bags bulged with guntheri, the small, sleek skink, and the Telfair skink. We were well satisfied.

We set off across the blue, gently undulating sea, leaving Round Island behind us ablaze in the setting sun. It looked more bleak and barren than ever, but now we knew the patches of palms and steep-sided ravines that gave blissful shade, the banks of tuff that provided wind-eroded homes for the Red-tailed tropic birds, the fronds of the palms decorated with geckos, and the bald, hot dome of the island alive with the quick, glittering shapes of the little skinks. We knew that under the picnic tree a host of eager, elegant Telfair skinks formed a welcoming committee, anxiously awaiting the next visiting humans. To us, the island was no longer just a chunk of barren volcanic debris, sun-drenched, sea-washed and wind-sculpted, but a living thing as important, as busy, as full of interest as a human village, peopled by charming and defenceless creatures eager to welcome one to their hot and inhospitable home.

The sea was calm and the sky without a shred or wisp of cloud, so that the sunset lay along the horizon like a glowing ingot of gold, fading gradually to green as the sun disappeared. Most of the party slept. Wahab, having consumed a pineapple, a cucumber and some cold curry, was promptly sick, went a peculiar shade of grey, curled up like a cat and went to sleep.

We drove back the long and bumpy ride to Black River, and there we laid the bags with our precious cargo on the cool floor of Dave's spare room and went tiredly to bed. The next morning we unpacked our catch and found, to our relief, that none of our captives was any the worse for their incarceration. The guntheri, velvety and glowering in a Churchillian manner, strolled nonchalantly into their cages. The little skinks skittered eagerly into their new environment, brisk, alert, each looking like the Salesman of the Year. The Telfairs were equally curious about their new home – a lavishly decorated aviary. We eased them out of their bags and they investigated every nook and cranny. Then, within five minutes, they were satisfied with their new quarters. They converged on us and, as if they had been born in captivity, climbed into our laps and accepted fat, black cockroaches and juicy lumps of banana from our fingers, in a most confiding and flattering way.

CHAPTER FOUR

THE FRUGIVOROUS FLIGHT

Wahab had stopped the car at a tiny shop where the owner and his entire family, from grandmother to youngest child, were absorbed in manufacturing chapatties and rolling them up with a filling of spiced lentils inside, by the light of glittering, yellow oil lamps. We purchased a goodly supply of these delicacies and then drove to the cool, moon-drenched hillside outside the town beneath a sky heavy with stars, where we sat and ate our chapatties and discussed our forthcoming bat-catching expedition to the neighbouring island of Rodrigues.

'You will have to take fruit with you, of course,' said Wahab wiping his fingers fastidiously on his handkerchief.

'Take fruit? What on earth for?' I asked, my mouth full of delicious chapatti. To take fruit to a tropical island seemed to me to be the Mascarene equivalent of taking coals to Newcastle.

'Well you see,' said Wahab, 'there is very little fruit grown in Rodrigues and, anyway, now it's the end of the fruit season.'

'It would be,' I said, ruefully.

'Isn't it going to be a bit of a problem?' asked John. 'I mean transporting fruit in a small plane.'

'No, no,' said Wahab, 'you just pack it up as if it's excess baggage, no trouble at all.'

'We'd better take some ripe, some medium, and some green,' I said, 'like you do on board ship to feed animals.'

'Yes,' said Wahab, 'and I will try and find you a Jak fruit.'

'What's a Jak fruit?' asked Ann.

'It's a large fruit that the bats are very, very fond of,' said Wahab. 'It has a strong smell, you see, and the bats can smell it from a distance.'

'Is it good eating?' I asked.

'Oh yes,' said Wahab, adding cautiously, 'if you like that sort of thing.'

By the time our trip to Rodrigues was over, I had come to look upon Jak fruit as one of the tropical delicacies least likely to succeed in any culinary contest but at that moment, I only had a mental image of a host of bats flying straight into our arms at the merest whiff of its delectable odour.

The next couple of days we spent checking our nets and other equipment, reading up on Rodrigues and, whenever possible, snorkelling on the reef, reviewing the multi-coloured ever-changing pageant of sea life that lived on or around it. News drifted to us that Wahab was having difficulty in getting Jak fruit and that Rodrigues was experiencing its first rainfall in eight years. Neither piece of gossip seemed of vital importance and yet, had we known it, both things were to affect our plans. Two days before we were due to fly to Rodrigues, Wahab phoned. He had, he said, tracked down positively the last Jak fruit on the island of Mauritius and had commandeered it for us. He was sending it round by special messenger.

'It's rather ripe, Gerry,' he explained, 'so you should keep it wrapped up so that it doesn't lose its scent, and keep it out of a high temperature.'

'How do you suggest I do that?' I enquired sarcastically, mopping the sweat from my brow. 'I can't even keep myself out of a high temperature.'

'Your hotel room is air conditioned, isn't it?' asked Wahab. 'Keep it there.'

'My hotel room already contains twenty-four hands of bananas, two dozen avocado pears, two dozen pineapples, two water melons and four dozen mangoes, purchased for this damned bat catching. It looks more like a market than the Port Louis market does; still, I suppose the addition of one Jak fruit won't make all that difference?'

That's right,' said Wahab, 'and, by the way, this sudden rain Rodrigues is having. It may affect your flight.'

'How?' I asked, suddenly filled with anxiety, for any delay would cut into the time we had allotted for the bat catching.

'Well, you know the airfield in Rodrigues is only an earth one.' explained Wahab. 'All this rain has made it very slippery. The plane yesterday had to turn back. Still, you may be all right.'

'Well, I hope to heaven we are,' I said, feeling depressed. 'If there's too much of a delay, we'll have to cancel our whole trip there.'

'Oh, I'm sure you won't have to do that,' said Wahab merrily.

'Let me know if there is anything else you want. The Jak fruit should be arriving later on in the morning. Goodbye.'

Telephone conversations with Wahab tended to begin and end abruptly.

The Jak fruit, wrapped up in swaddling clothes of polythene and sacking, arrived in the arms of a smartly uniformed forest guard at about midday. Judging by the size of the parcel, a Jak fruit was considerably bigger than I had imagined. I had visualised it as being about the size of a coconut, but this fruit was obviously as big as a large marrow. The parcel had, during its travels, got very hot and I took it into the bedroom and reverently unwrapped it so as to let the cool air get at its contents. What was revealed, when the swaddling clothes were stripped away, was an obscene green fruit covered with knobs and looking rather like the corpse of a Martian baby. To help the illusion, there arose from it a thick, sweetish, very pungent smell, vaguely reminiscent of a putrefying body.

I was to learn, as time progressed, that this sickly cloying scent permeated everything and insinuated itself everywhere, rather as paraffin does when left in untutored hands. Within an astonishingly short space of time, the whole room smelt like a gigantic Jak fruit, or a morgue where the freezing unit has developed a fault. Our clothes smelt of Jak fruit, as did our shoes; the books, cameras, binoculars; the suitcases and the bat-catching nets. You escaped from the room in order to snatch a breath of fresh air, only to find you had taken the smell with you. The whole landscape was redolent of Jak fruit. In an effort to elude this all-pervading scent, we went snorkelling on the reef and it smelt as though we had Jak fruits imprisoned in our masks. Our lunch tasted entirely of Jak fruit, as did dinner. Breakfast, heavily impregnated with Jak fruit, made me glad that we were flying to Rodrigues that day, where we could

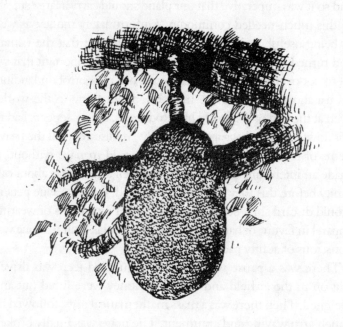

leave this diabolical fruit in the forest and perhaps escape its effluvium.

We arrived at the airport and within minutes, the departure lounge smelt so strongly of Jak fruit that all the other passengers started to cough and glance about them uneasily. We were a motley enough looking crew to arouse thoughts of hi-jacking, with our incomprehensible bundles of nets and baskets bulging with a weird assortment of fruit, in the midst of which the Jak fruit lay and simmered in its baby clothes of sacking and polythene.

Presently, it was time to check in, and we discovered how the first rainfall for eight years in Rodrigues – desirable though it might be for the island – was detrimental to our cause. Apparently, as well as a shortage of rain, Rodrigues had a dearth of money and so it was imperative that our plane should carry a large supply of this much-needed commodity. Unfortunately money, as well as being useful, weighs a lot. Owing to the fact that the rainfall had turned the airfield into a quagmire, it was important that we were not overweight lest the plane get out of control on landing. As usual, money being the most important thing in the world, even at the end of the world like Rodrigues, the passengers had to cut down on their baggage. Frantically, we discarded all the heavy items of clothing and equipment we could manage without. It made an interesting pile. If there had been any doubts about our sanity before this they were soon dispelled, for what sane person would discard shirt, socks, shoes and other vital items of wearing apparel in favour of bananas, mangoes and a Jak fruit that one was conscious of at fifty paces?

There was a pause while a heavily guarded jeep was driven out on to the airfield and boxes of money were lifted out and weighed. Then there was a mass mathematical orgy, followed by much arm waving and argument. The news was finally broken to us that, in spite of our sacrifice we were still overweight. To the evident satisfaction of the man in charge of Weights and Measures, we sat down and ate half our fruit, It was lunch time anyway. Just as we were feeling we never wanted to eat another banana, it was announced that the flight was cancelled owing to the state of the runway in Rodrigues. Would we all kindly report at the same time tomorrow?

Taking our, by now almost lethal, Jak fruit, we drove back to the hotel. They were not overjoyed to see us since they had only just succeeded in getting the smell of the Jak fruit out of the bedrooms. The following day, having replaced our now rotting fruit with fresh, we reported once more to the airport. For some strange reason, we had to be weighed in again, as did the money. They found we were overweight. It was at this point that I began to have serious doubts about the mathematical abilities of the Mauritians but, as anyone knows who has tried it, it is useless arguing with an airport official. We sat down, having discarded virtually everything but the clothes we stood up in and our nets, and ate some more of our precious fruit. The fact that we were now carrying the extra weight within us, rather than in hands of bananas, did not appear to perturb the airport officials at all. The temptation to discard the Jak fruit was immense but even I realised its pungency might prove useful in luring the bats into our nets, provided it did not asphyxiate us or them first. We had just consumed another glut of bananas when they told us that the flight was cancelled again.

'If this is an example of how the Rodrigues trip is going to go, I shall have a very upset stomach,' I said, as we arrived back at the hotel, where they viewed our reappearance with a long-suffering air. I was genuinely worried, for if there was one more delay, we would have to cancel the whole Rodrigues venture. It was getting close to our departure date for Europe. The following day, having replaced all the bananas and mangoes which had become over-ripe and, for the hundredth time, wished we had an airtight box for the Jak fruit, we went to the airport once more. Again we and the money were laboriously weighed but this time, to our astonishment, we were not forced to eat half of our luggage. Soon we found ourselves on board the tiny plane with a motley assortment of passengers, who viewed the arrival of the Jak fruit in that confined space with a certain alarm and despondency. The soldiers who had been guarding the plane now dispersed, and we taxied down the runway and took off, flying low over the vivid green patchwork of sugar cane and rising higher and higher into the hyacinth-blue sky, as we flew across the reef and out over the deep, sparkling blue of the Indian Ocean.

Rodrigues lies a little over 350 miles east of Mauritius, well out into the Indian Ocean; an island eleven miles long and five-and-a-quarter miles wide at its widest point. It has had an interesting history and a still more interesting fauna. One of these was that strange bird, the Solitaire, which had evolved on the island. This bird became extinct shortly after the Dodo and the reason for its demise appears to have been the destruction of its habitat, as well as ruthless hunting. Together with the Solitaire, the island was shared by a species of giant tortoise, of which there were a prodigious number. In his fascinating book on Rodrigues, Alfred North-Coombes goes into the exploitation of these tortoises:

Giant tortoises take thirty to forty years to reach maturity and may live for as long as two to three hundred years. It was only the isolated position of these islands, the absence of man and natural enemies, which favoured this development to an almost fabulous extent. Indeed, Leguat says that they were so numerous at Rodrigues 'that sometimes you see two or three thousand of them in a flock; so that you may go above a hundred paces on their backs... without setting foot to ground.'

Thus, by the time Mahé de Labourdonnais arrived at Isle de France, thousands of tortoises had already been removed from Rodrigues for Bourbon, Isle de France and the Company's ships. The latter plundered indiscriminately, often far beyond the essential requirements of their crews and passengers. Some captains sold the surplus at Bourbon where apparently the demand was greater and the price good, refusing even to let Isle de France have some for the sick of other vessels. Labourdonnais exclaims: 'Would you believe it, Sir, there are captains who come from Rodrigues with seven to eight hundred tortoises, who refuse to land them here for the sick of other ships, preferring to sell them at Bourbon or exchange them there for chickens!'

Labourdonnais did not keep an exact account of the number of tortoises removed from Rodrigues during his governorship. It could hardly have been less than 10,000 annually. One of his successors, Desforges-Bourcher, the same who was formerly governor of Bourbon and had attempted to establish a colony at Rodrigues in 1725, was more precise. Four little ships were engaged during his governorship in transporting the tortoises to Isle de France. They were *La Mignonne*, *L'Oiseau*, *Le Volant* and *Le Pénélope*. Thousands of tortoises were brought back each time, as the following extract from one of his reports to the Company shows:

14 December 1759
L'Oiseau arrives from Rodrigues with 1035 tortoises and 47 turtles. She had loaded 5000, but took eight days to reach Isle de France and lost most of the cargo.

15 May 1760
– *L'Oiseau* brings 6000 tortoises

29 September 1760
– *L'Oiseau* arrives with 1600 tortoises and 171 turtles

12 May 1761
– *Le Volant* docks with a cargo of 4000 tortoises

6 December 1761
– *L'Oiseau* brings 3800 tortoises alive out of a shipment of 5000.

The Royal Navy helped itself too, when in Rodrigues waters.
Thus on 26 July 1761 two ships loaded 3000 tortoises.

Presently, after two-and-a-half hours' flying, we saw ahead of
us the meandering, ever-moving scarf of ivory-white foam
that marked the reef around Rodrigues. This great bastion of
coral ringed the island and, indeed, formed a great shelf in the
deep ocean on which the island stood. The reef in some places
was twenty miles from the island's shore and the great piece of
placid, emerald green water it guarded was dotted with smaller
islands, some mere sand dunes, others substantial enough to
have given refuge to giant tortoises and a giant species of lizard,
also now extinct. We banked and came in low to land on the
tiny, red earth airfield. From the air, the island looked biscuit-
brown and pretty barren, though there were patches of green in
the valleys and a scattering of dusty green vegetation elsewhere.
From the moment we left the plane, we were enveloped in the
magic charms one only feels on small, remote, sun-illuminated
islands. We made our way over the red laterite airstrip and into
the minute airport building, on the facade of which was the
heartwarming sign saying 'Welcome to Rodrigues'. Inside, I saw,
to my astonishment, a desk set in an open window on which
there was a sign saying 'Immigration'.

'Immigration?' I said to John. 'What can they mean?
They've only one plane a week from Réunion and three from
Mauritius.'

'Don't ask me,' he said, 'perhaps it's not for us.'

'Please to have passports ready for Immigration,' said a jovial
policeman in smart green uniform, thus dispelling any doubt.

It was fortunate we had by chance brought our passports with
us, since it had not occurred to us that we would need them,
Rodrigues being a dependency of Mauritius. At that moment,

the Immigration Officer himself arrived; a large, chocolate-coloured Rodriguan in a handsome, khaki uniform. He was sweating profusely and carried a big bundle of unruly files. He had an earnest, nervous, wrinkled face like a bloodhound recovering from a nervous breakdown. He seated himself at the desk, knocked over the sign saying 'Immigration Officer' with his files, and smiled at us nervously as he righted it. We lined up in front of him, dutifully brandishing our passports. He gave us a little bow, cleared his throat and then, with a flourish, opened a file which contained immigration forms of the sort that ask you every imaginably fatuous question, from your date of birth to whether your grandmother had ingrowing toenails. His stern demeanour as an upholder of the law was slightly undermined when a gust of warm air from the window blew his forms all over what, for want of a better term, one must call the airport lounge. We all scrabbled around collecting them for him and he was pathetically grateful.

He was now sweating even more profusely than before. He leant his rotund elbows on the forms to prevent another unfortunate episode, and took Ann's passport. Laboriously he copied out her place and date of birth, her age and her profession. This was all plain sailing and he handed her back her passport with a wide glittering, triumphant smile; the smile of a man who has the situation under control. His confidence was premature, however, for, flushed with enthusiasm, he leant forward to take my passport and another sly gust of wind scattered his forms like confetti across the airport lounge. It took several minutes to retrieve them all and by that time Ann's form had a handsome boot mark on it where a helpful member of the airport police had stamped on it as it slid past him along the floor.

We re-established the Immigration Officer at his desk and he accepted, with gratitude, Ann's offer that she stood behind him and held down his migratory paper forms while he devoted his time to filling them in. Rid of the burden of this paperwork, as it were, he was now free to show his mettle as Immigration Officer. He took my passport and riffled it with his chocolate-coloured fingers like an expert card sharper. He gave me what I think was supposed to be a shrewd and penetrating glance, but it was far too beguiling to be this.

'Where have you come from?' he asked.

As Rodrigues had been waterlogged for two weeks and we were the first plane in from Mauritius in that time and as there was only that plane on the airport, I found the question baffling. If it had been made to me at London Airport, say, with hundreds of planes an hour coming in, it would have had some relevance, but here in Rodrigues with, at best, only four planes a week the question took on a slightly 'Looking-Glass' quality. I resisted the impulse to say that I had just swum ashore, and told him instead that I had come from Mauritius. He puzzled over the 'author/zoologist' designation under 'Occupation' in my passport, obviously thinking it might be something as dangerous as CIA or MI5; then, with some difficulty over the 'zoologist', he copied it out slowly and carefully on to his form. Then he stamped my passport and handed it back to me, with his ingratiating smile, and I made way for John. Meanwhile, Ann was having a struggle with the forms, as quite a stiff breeze had sprung up. She was now helped in her task by the policeman who had contributed his boot mark to her form. He seemed determined that the police force should not be lagging behind the immigration authorities in devotion to duty.

The immigration man now took John's passport and asked him where he had come from.

'Yorkshire, in England,' said John innocently, before I could stop him.

'No, no,' said the immigration man, confused by this largesse of information, 'I mean where you come from now?'

'Oh,' said John, 'Mauritius.'

The immigration man wrote it down carefully. He opened John's passport and laboriously copied out the relevant information regarding John's nascence. Then he looked at John's occupation and saw the dreaded and incomprehensible word 'herpetologist'. His eyes shut and his face wrinkled in alarm. He looked like a man who every night for years has awoken, screaming, from a dream in which his superiors have not only asked him to define what a 'herpetologist' was but to spell it as well. Now his dream had come true. He licked his lips, opened his eyes, and glanced nervously at the dreaded word, hoping it had gone away. It stared back at him implacably, unununderstandable and unspellable. He made a valiant attempt.

'Herpa... er... Herper...' he said, and looked desperately at the policeman for help. The policeman leant over his shoulder and glanced at the word that was confusing his colleague, with the amused air of one for whom *The Times* crossword puzzle is child's play, then his eyes alighted on 'herpetologist' and he became less confident.

'Herp... herp...' he said, dolefully and unhelpfully.

'Herpa... herper...' said the immigration man.

'Herp... herp... herp...' said the policeman.

It began to sound like one of the lesser-known, and more incomprehensible German operas.

'Herpetologist,' I said, briskly.

'Ah, yes,' said the Immigration Officer, wisely.

'What is that?' asked the policeman, more bluntly.

'It means someone who studies snakes,' I explained.

He gazed at the word, fascinated.

'You have come here to study snakes?' asked the policeman, at last, with the air of one humouring a dangerous lunatic.

'Here, there are no snakes,' said his colleague, speaking with the authority of one who would never let a snake wriggle through Immigration if he could help it.

'Well, no, we've come here to catch bats,' I said, incautiously.

They stared at me, disbelievingly.

'Bats?' asked the policeman.

'Bats is not snakes,' said the Immigration Officer, with the air of Charles Darwin giving the fruits of his life's researches to the world.

'No, I know,' I said, 'but we have come here at the invitation of the Commissioner, Mr Hazeltine, to catch bats.' I felt sure that Mr Hazeltine, whom I had never met, would forgive me this innocent falsehood. Both the policeman and the immigration man nearly stood to attention at the mention of the Commissioner's name.

'You know Mr Hazeltine?' asked the immigration man.

'He asked us to come,' I said, simply.

The immigration man knew when he was beaten. He laboriously and carefully spelt out 'Herpetologist', stamped John's passport and smiled at us with evident relief. We shook hands with him and the helpful policeman, and as we did so, they wished us a happy stay in Rodrigues. I wondered why it was necessary to burden a simple, straightforward and happy island people with a bureaucracy that was so out of place and so futile in such a setting.

We got into the hotel jeep and were driven along the winding roads, through an eroded and desiccated landscape. Here and there the edges of the road were green and there were pockets of dusty trees and bushes around ramshackle, corrugated iron huts. The driver assured us that, after its recent rainfall, the island was green. I wondered, looking at the dry and dusty landscape under the fierce sun, what it had looked like before.

Eventually, the jeep edged its way down the one main street of Port Mathurin, the metropolis of Rodrigues. This was edged with a scrappy collection of wooden and corrugated iron houses and shops, but its length was as bright as a flower bed with the inhabitants of the port dressed in their bright clothes, busy about their shopping. A little outside the port, the jeep came to a standstill and there, on the crest of the hill above us, was the hotel. It was a low structure with a broad, steeply-pitched roof covering a deep, shady verandah that surrounded the building. This verandah was approached by wide steps and had complicated, wrought iron railings, painted white, running round its length. On the verandah were scattered tables and long cane chairs. The hotel, perched on the hilltop, commanded a view of the whole of Port Mathurin and the reef some three miles away. It resembled nothing so much as a rather exaggerated film set for a Somerset Maugham story, and this atmosphere was enhanced by the steep path leading up to it, flanked by hibiscus bushes covered with large magenta and orange flowers, that looked like paper cutouts, and a herd of slightly grubby, but most attentive and welcoming pigs that were holding a convention under and around the hotel itself.

Once we had established ourselves and made contact with Mr Hazeltine, the Commissioner, who lived in an imposing old residence, surrounded by massive trees loaded with epiphytes within a walled garden and whose gate was guarded by a belligerent-looking cannon, we contacted Mr Marie, the Head of the Forestry Department, and he offered to drive us out to view the bats. According to him, the bat colony resided in the valley of Cascade Pigeon, some three miles away from

Port Mathurin. He thought that there might be two or three odd specimens living a solitary existence in other parts of the island, but he was sure that the bulk of the colony was in this valley. So we piled into his Land-Rover and, together with young Jean Claude Rabaude, a Forest worker, who was also a keen amateur naturalist and who had helped Anthony Cheke on his expedition, we drove out to the valley.

When we got there, we parked the jeep and made our way down the rocky, slippery slope, along a path that resembled nothing so much as a stream bed. Presently, about halfway to the bottom of the valley, we came on to a rocky promontory that commanded a view up the valley slope to the left. Here the trees were fairly low, some twenty feet in height, but in their midst grew a number of very large mango trees. It was these tall trees, with their broad, glossy, shade-giving leaves, that constituted the roosting area for the bats.

At first glance through the binoculars it appeared that each mango tree had produced a strange crop of furry fruit, chocolate brown and golden red, but as the bats yawned and stretched, you could see the leather, umbrella-like wings were dark chocolate brown, while the fur on the bodies and heads ranged from bright, glittering yellow, like spun gold, to a deep fox red. They were, without doubt, the most colourful and handsome fruit bats I had ever seen. They had rounded heads with small, neat ears and short, somewhat blunt muzzles that made them look like pomeranians. The bulk of the colony hung in these three mango trees, and solitary individuals roosted in the smaller trees around.

Having located the colony, we had to try to assess its numbers with some degree of accuracy. As many bats were roosting deep in the shady mango trees, they were not always visible and as, periodically, one or more bats would fly from one mango tree to another, or simply flap their way in a leisurely fashion across the hillside and back again, the count presented problems. First of all, the five of us counted the colony from where we stood, and we took a number mid-way between all our estimates. We felt this was fairly haphazard, since a lot of bats were on the move, but even so we were encouraged by the fact that two of us had counted more than the number that Anthony Cheke had estimated two years previously.

According to Jean Claude, who was convinced that the colony had increased substantially since Cheke's day, the best time for counting – that is, when the bats were the stillest – was first thing in the morning when they had just arrived back from their night feed, and at noon when the sun was hottest. As it was only eleven o dock, we decided to wait until noon and count again. In the meantime, we looked round for a suitable spot in which to set up the net, should we decide to catch any bats.

It was John who found the perfect glade, a clearing facing down towards the valley, surrounded by big trees which were ideal for slinging the nets from, and which provided us with maximum shelter from the sun. In the torrid quiet of noon, we counted the bats again. They were very still now, with only the occasional movement when they spread their dark wings and flapped them to keep cool. We counted over one hundred. Greatly elated, but determined to be cautious, I sent John round to the other side of the valley with Jean Claude to do another count. Then, to make finally sure, we counted them flying from the roost that night and again the next morning. Our final estimate was that the colony consisted of between one hundred and twenty and one hundred and thirty individuals, certainly not an impressive number but heartening, nevertheless, as it meant that the colony had increased by some thirty-five specimens since Cheke counted them.

Thus encouraged, we decided that the maximum number we could take without damaging the survival chances of the colony and the minimum number we needed for successful breeding groups was eighteen specimens. As with most animals which lived in colonies, I felt that the bats would need the stimulus of their own kind about them if they were to settle down and breed successfully, therefore, it was useless thinking in terms of one pair or even two pairs. The numbers had to give the impression of a colony, albeit a small one. But it is one thing to decide how many and what sexes of an animal you are going to catch, even if you know where it is; quite another to accomplish this successfully.

The clearing we had chosen for our operations was about a quarter of a mile from the colony, and lay on the route down the valley which they seemed to take when flying off to feed each evening. When they actually flew down the valley, it was at a slightly lower level than the clearing but here I was hoping that the Jak fruit (now making the hotel unique as a hostelry) would come into its own and lure the bats up to our level.

The method of capture we chose was simplicity itself. With the aid of Jean Claude and a compatriot (who distressed my intrepid explorer's instincts by wearing a tee shirt emblazoned with the words 'I dig President Kennedy') we hitched up some eight mist nets to the trees so that they formed a hollow square or box, some fifty feet by seventy feet, with walls about forty feet high. Then, out of wire netting, we built something that looked like a miniature coffin, heavily disguised with branches, and slung it in readiness in the centre of the nets. This was to be the repository for the fruit. Thus, having organised everything satisfactorily, we sped back to the hotel, had a hasty meal and returned to the valley, armed with torches and fruit, just as the twilight was turning greenish, preparatory to fading into grey.

The bats were waking up, getting ready for their nightly sortie for food. They were more vocal and they kept taking off from the mango trees and flying in anxious circles round it before settling again. It was obvious that it was not quite dark enough for them yet. We stuffed our wire coffin with over-ripe mangoes, bananas and pineapples, and then I approached the Jak fruit with a machete. Without waiting for it to protest, I split it in twain lengthways, and then wished I had not done so. I had believed that it was impossible for the smell of this endearing fruit to get any stronger, but I was wrong. Within seconds, apparently, the whole of Rodrigues smelt strongly of Jak fruit. Hoping the bats would appreciate it, even if we did not, we stuffed the fruit into the coffin and hauled the whole thing up until, in its shroud of branches, it hung some twenty feet up in the centre of the nets. Then we found ourselves a suitable hiding place in the bushes overlooking the trap, and settled down to wait. Unfortunately, owing to the fact that we had been forced to discard most of our clothing in an effort to save weight, we were all clad in shorts and short-sleeved shirts, a garb that did not help us when approximately three-quarters of the mosquito population of Rodrigues decided to join us in our vigil.

So we waited, our cars ringing with the shrill, excited, friendly cries of the mosquitoes, while the green twilight faded into grey and then an even darker shade. Just before it became too dark to see, the bats started to flight. They flew singly, or in little groups of three or four, heading down the valley towards Port Mathurin. As they flapped across the sky at the edge of our clearing, they looked astonishingly big and their slow, heavy flight made them resemble something out of a Dracula movie. With praise-worthy single-mindedness, they flew down the valley, not deviating to right or left, and completely ignoring us, our nets and our odoriferous bait of overripe fruit. We sat there in a haze of mosquitoes, scratching ourselves and glowering at the passing stream of bats. Presently, the stream thinned to a trickle and then to the odd late risers, flapping hurriedly after the bulk of the colony. Soon there were no bats at all. Not one of them had displayed the faintest interest in our Jak-fruit-permeated clearing.

'Well, this is jolly,' said John, stretching his lanky form out of one of the bushes, like a wounded giraffe. 'I'm rather glad we came really, I would hate to think of all these mosquitoes going hungry.'

'Yes, it's a form of conservation programme really,' I said. 'You can imagine how many mosquitoes we have saved from starvation tonight. In years to come, the World Wildlife Fund will probably erect a posthumous Golden Ark on this spot to commemorate our contribution to nature.'

'It's all very well for you to joke,' said Ann, bitterly. 'You don't seem to be affected when they bite you, whereas I itch like hell and then swell up and go red.'

'Never mind,' I said, soothingly, 'just close your eyes and try to work out what we are going to do with all those bats we are going to catch.'

Ann grunted derisively. After a couple of hours, when no bats had appeared and when the mosquitoes had returned for the main course, as it were, we held a council of war. I felt it was important that at least one of us should stay there all night in case a bat or bats returned and got caught. The nets were slung up in such a complicated way that it was impossible to lower them, and I did not want any bats to hang in the nets all night, should one be caught. After some discussion, we all decided to stay and made ourselves as comfortable as we could among the bushes, having decided that one would keep watch, while the others slept.

Then, in the early hours of the morning, the rain began. There was no warning, no thunder, no lightning, none of those brash preliminaries. There was suddenly a roar like an avalanche of steel ball-bearings as the clouds parted and dropped rain on us with the concentrated fury of a suddenly opened flood gate. Within seconds, we were soaked and sitting in what appeared to be the opening stages of a waterfall, that had all the promise of growing into something like Niagara. The rain, in contrast to the hot, steamy night, felt as if it had newly emerged from some glacier, and we shivered with cold. We removed from the bushes to a spot under the tree as this afforded us a little more shelter; the leaves were being machine-gunned by huge raindrops and the water was running in streams down the tree trunks.

We stood it for an hour, then an investigation proved that the sky over the whole island was black and stretched, as far as we could make out, from Cascade Pigeon across the Indian Ocean to Delhi. It was obvious that no self-respecting bat was going to fly around in that torrential downpour, so we packed up our dripping equipment and made our way back to the hotel where we could at least shelter from the rain and the mosquitoes, and snatch two or three hours' sleep. We were determined to be back at the nets at dawn, for this was when the bats would return from their feeding grounds and might conceivably blunder into our nets.

Dawn saw us, stiff and half-asleep, crouched under the nets, in a strange green light. The whole forest smelt warm and as redolent as a fruit cake freshly made from an oven. The scents of the earth and moss and leaves, air-warmed and rain-washed, were strong enough but transcending all these subtle olfactory treats was the bugle-blast of the Jak fruit, slung some twenty feet above us. Presently, the sky lightened and soon the bats reappeared, flapping languidly back to their roost. A number had passed us when, to our excitement, several veered away from what could be described as the flight path and circled over our clearing in a suspicious, but interested manner, before flapping off to the mango tree. Encouraged by this show of interest, we spent the day rigging up more nets among the trees, helped by sudden downpours of rain.

Our two helpers from the Forestry Department, shocked by the fact that we had been out all night during one of the heaviest rainstorms Rodrigues had experienced in eight years, cut poles and banana leaves and constructed for us, well concealed in the bushes, a small banana-leaf hut, something a Congo pigmy might have considered a baronial hall. You cannot, however, look gift huts in the mouth and we decided that, if John left half his legs outside, it would provide us with adequate shelter against the weather.

We took the precaution of visiting the inevitable Chinese stores in Port Mathurin – there did not appear to be any other kind of store – and purchased some plastic sheeting and a few cheap blankets. When dark fell, and the bats had flown past us again, after some considerable argument, it was decided that Ann should go back to the hotel and get a decent night's sleep and join us again at dawn. When she had departed, John and I made up makeshift beds of plastic sheeting and blankets in our banana-leaf cottage, and arranged our accoutrements – a good supply of sandwiches and chocolate; a Thermos of tea; torches; and a hopeful clutch of small, but delightful, wicker baskets, called Tantes, which are one of Rodrigues's chief exports, and in which we hoped to incarcerate our catch of bats. We tossed for who should keep the first watch and I won, so I curled up happily and was soon asleep.

When it was my turn to assume sentry duty, I went for a short walk around the clearing to stretch my legs. The earth and vegetation were still saturated with moisture, although it had not rained for some hours, and the air was warm and so water-laden that each breath you took made you feel as though your lungs were absorbing moisture like a sponge. On the fallen and rotting branches that lay about, I found innumerable small, phosphorescent fungi that glowed with a bright greenish-blue light, so that part of the forest floor was illuminated like a city seen from the air at night. I collected some of these twigs and branches, and found that ten or twelve of these glowing fungi produced enough light to be able to read by, providing you kept your light source fairly close to the page.

It was while I was attempting to read by the light of the fungi that I heard a curious sound that seemed to emanate from the forest behind our little hut. It was a fairly loud scrunching noise. It sounded to me, for some bizarre reason, like a matchbox being crushed in the hands of a very powerful man. Reluctantly I was forced to admit that, eccentric though the Rodriguans might be, it was unlikely that they crept about rain-drenched forests at three in the morning crushing matchboxes. Taking a torch, I eased my way out of our fragile hut and went to investigate. This was not quite so intrepid as it may appear, since there is nothing harmful in the animal line in Rodrigues, if you ignore the human animal. I made a careful search of the forest behind the hut, but could find nothing living that looked as though its normal cry resembled the crushing of a matchbox, and met nothing more ferocious than a large moth which seemed intent on trying to fly up the barrel of my torch. I went back to the hut and sat there, thinking. I wondered if we would catch any bats in the morning. Time was running short and I was debating with myself whether to move the nets nearer to the colony's roosting site. As I was pondering this problem, I was startled by the rasping matchbox noise again, this time very much closer and from several different directions. John, who had woken up, sat up and stared at me.

'What's that?' he enquired, sleepily.

'I haven't the faintest idea, but it's been going on for about ten minutes. I had a look round and I couldn't see anything.'

Just then, there was a positive battery of rasping noises, and the walls and the roof of the hut started to vibrate.

'What the hell can it be?' asked John.

I shone my torch at the banana-leaf roof and saw it was quivering and swaying, as though in an earthquake.

Before we could do anything intelligent, the whole roof gave way and a cascade of giant landsnails, each the size of a small apple, descended upon us. They were fat, glossy and wet, and they gleamed in the torchlight, frothing gently and leaving an interesting pattern of slime on our beds. It took us ten minutes to rid our shelter of these unwanted gastropods and to repair the roof. John curled up and went to sleep again, and I sat wondering if the bats, perhaps, had the same feeling about the Jak fruit as I had, and that this was why we had not met with success. An hour later, John woke up and claimed he was hungry.

'I think I'll have a sandwich or two,' he said, 'can you bung some over to me?'

I switched on the torch and shone it in the corner of the shelter that acted as our commissariat. To my dismay, I saw that all the giant landsnails we had so painstakingly evicted from our hut had silently and surreptitiously returned, and now formed a glittering, amber pile on our sandwiches, eating the bread with evident relish. They were aided and abetted by a half-grown, grey rat with glossy fur, white paws, and a forest of black whiskers. The snails were not alarmed by the torchlight and continued browsing happily on our supper, but the rat was of a more nervous disposition. As the torch beam hit him, he froze for an instant, only his whiskers quivering and his eyes rolling; then, with a piercing soprano scream, he turned round and rushed straight under the blanket into bed with me. He seemed convinced that this was a haven of safety, and I dislodged him with considerable difficulty by taking my bed to pieces. Having shooed him out of the hut and into the forest, I then retrieved the remainder of the sandwiches from the snails and while John was sorting out the less ragged and more edible ones, I banished the snails once more to the outer edges of the clearing. An hour or so later, John woke up again and claimed himself still hungry.

'You can't be still hungry,' I said, 'you only had some sandwiches an hour ago.'

'I only had what the snails had left,' said John, aggrievedly. 'Didn't we have some biscuits? Biscuits and a cup of tea. That would be nice.'

Sighing, I switched on the torch and, to my amazement, found the identical scene in our kitchen area. The snails had oozed their way back and were now feeding on the biscuits, as was my friend, the rat. Once again, as the torchlight hit him, the latter uttered his hysterical scream and dived into bed with me; this time, presumably so that I could give him even greater protection, he tried to climb up inside my shorts. I banished him with some firmness into the forest, hurled the snails after him, and removed the remainder of our food over to John's side of the hut. I felt it was his turn to get on intimate terms with the rat. By this time, of course, we were so wide awake that we could not get to sleep, so sat and talked in a desultory fashion, waiting for it to get light. Just before dawn, we heard Ann stumbling through the forest towards us.

'Caught anything?' she asked when she arrived.

'No,' I said, 'if you discount snails and a rat. But we might get something when it gets lighter.'

Gradually, the sky paled primrose yellow and the light strengthened as we left our snail-eaten hut and moved down to the trees nearer the nets.

'I can't understand why they don't come,' I said. 'They must be able to smell that damned Jak fruit in Chicago!'

'I know,' said John, 'what I think is...'

But what he thought was never vouchsafed to us, for he leant forward, peering intently.

'What's that?' he said, pointing. 'Surely it's something in the net. Is it a bat?'

We all strained our eyes, staring into the clearing where the mist nets, fine as gossamer, vanished against the trees and shadows.

'Yes,' said Ann, excitedly, 'I can see it. I'm sure it's a bat.'

'I think you're right,' I said, 'but how the hell did he get in there without us knowing?'

At that moment, a bat entered the clearing, did a swift and cautious investigation and then flew away, demonstrating first of all the complete silence of its approach and, secondly, the fact that from where our hut was, higher up the hill, we could not have seen it, for once it entered the clearing, it vanished into the broken shadows.

By now, the light had strengthened considerably and, to our excitement, we could see not one, but ten bats hanging in the nets. To say that we were elated was putting it mildly, for, secretly, I think all of us had felt our chances of success were slight.

The bats were hanging, immobile, in the nets and as they were not struggling and panicking, we decided to wait for a while and see if we caught any more before releasing them. Several

bats flew into the clearing during the next half-hour, but they were too cautious and kept too high to get entangled in the mist nets. At length, it became obvious that we were not going to catch any more, and so we got our supply of Tantes ready and set about the task of disentangling the ones we had caught.

First of all, we sexed them. To our irritation, they were all males. They were even more beautiful close to than from a distance, for their backs were a bright chestnut fox red, changing to glittering spun gold on the shoulders and belly. The soot black wings were as fine and soft as chamois leather. Their funny little, chubby, golden faces with pale, straw-coloured yellow eyes, made them look like strange, indignant, miniature, flying teddy bears. The fine mesh of the net had done a good job and the delicate wings of each bat were intricately entangled; after spending a quarter of an hour trying to free one wing unsuccessfully, we gave up and simply cut the animals loose.

Even this had to be done with great care to make sure you did not cut or tear the delicate wing membrane, and at the same time we tried to do as little damage as possible to the net.

It was a difficult job, not made any easier by the anger of the bats, who seized every opportunity to sink their needle-sharp teeth into unwary fingers. But, at last, we had cut them all loose without doing too much damage to the nets, and placed them safely in individual Tantes. Then we attended to the laborious business of mending the nets and re-hanging them aloft again. By this time, our two helpers had arrived to take over the day shift, and were vastly amused by our story of the house and the sandwich-eating snails. They set about rebuilding our banana-leaf shelter. We left them, promising to return in the evening, and carried our bats in triumph down to Port Mathurin.

The local school, with extreme generosity, had offered us a newly-built classroom – as yet untenanted by the knowledge-hungry youth of Rodrigues – in which to keep our bats. It was a room some twenty feet by ten feet, newly painted and decorated, and ideal, as far as we were concerned, for keeping bats in. We had decked it out with plenty of branches and various hanging trays of wire on which we were going to serve the galaxy of fruit we had brought from Mauritius. We decided that we would let all the males we had caught loose in the room, and keep any females we got in Tantes. Lest I be accused of being a Chauvinist Pig, let me hasten to say that this apparent discrimination was due entirely to the fact that the females we got would be immensely more valuable than the males, and so we would have to be very careful with them.

Late in the afternoon, we returned to the glade and our two faithful bat watchers. In the fading afternoon light, we climbed to our vantage point in the valley and watched the colony. By and large, there was little movement, although the bats slept fitfully and frequently, and with great agility changed sleeping positions, moving through the branches with the aid of the hooks on their wings, with extraordinary skill. Only occasionally did one take flight and flap languidly round, before returning to the same roost or finding a new one.

On the whole, the colony was very silent; there was occasional bickering when a bat got too close to one of its sleeping compatriots, but this was seldom.

There was, however, one bat in the colony that was far from silent. It was a fat baby that we had christened 'Ambrose', and he was being weaned by his mother and was not taking kindly to the process. Although he was almost as big as she was he did not see why he should not cling to her as he had always done, nor why he should give up suckling whenever he felt like it. His mother, however, was being firm about it and his rage and petulance were horrible to hear. Screeching and twittering, he pursued his unfortunate mother from branch to branch, endeavouring to pull her within range with the hooks on his wings, and letting out outraged shrieks of frustration when he failed. The only let-up to this awful noise came when his mother, nerves cracking under the strain, would take flight and settle in a tree some distance away. Then Ambrose would stop screaming briefly, because he was concentrating all his efforts on screwing up the courage to fly after her. Eventually he would join her and as soon as he had recovered from the journey, his whining and importuning would start all over again.

'What a ghastly bat,' said Ann, 'I'd slaughter it if it were mine.'

'It needs to be sent to a public school,' said John, judiciously.

'A reform school would be better,' suggested Ann.

'All I can say is that I hope we don't, by some mischance, catch it in the nets. If we do, it will be one we will certainly let go, even if it's female,' I said.

'Too true,' said John. 'Imagine having that screeching around you all day.'

When it grew dark, we moved down to our banana-leaf home and spent the night with some persistent giant snails, several million mosquitoes, and one or two large and belligerent centipedes. The rat did not visit us, and I can only suppose he was in his burrow having a nervous breakdown. In the morning, we found we had caught two more bats and these, to our delight, proved to be females. We cut them loose and transported them carefully to the schoolroom, where our previous captives had settled down very well. The floor was deep in guano, and there was fruit everywhere.

We were booked to leave on the flight to Mauritius that took off at two o'clock the following day, so this meant that we had to catch our full quota of bats early that morning. It was obviously going to be touch and go, but in the green light of dawn, to our relief, we saw that we had caught thirteen bats and that among them were the females we required. In all, we had caught twenty-five bats; seven of the males we were going to release. Having extracted the thirteen bats from the nets and put them in their individual Tantes, we folded up the nets and for the last time climbed up the rocky path, out of Cascade Pigeon. As we left, we could hear Ambrose still screeching imploringly to his mother. That was one bat who was determined not to become extinct if he could help it!

When we got to the schoolroom, we had to go through the process of checking on all the male bats and picking out the right proportion of fully adult and of younger males, so that we would have the right age balance in our colonies. This done, we gathered up all the surplus males in Tantes and drove out of town to the beginning of the Cascade

Pigeon to let them go. We chose a really high vantage point and threw the bats, one at a time, into the air. They all turned towards the colony further up the valley. There was quite a stiff breeze blowing down the valley, and it was interesting to note that the bats flying against it made very heavy weather and had to land in the trees frequently for a rest. We wondered how they would fare in a cyclone lasting three or four days, or a week.

So, eventually, we had all our bats in their individual Tantes and we drove down to the airport. The immigration and police waved us a cheerful farewell as we loaded our strange cargo on to the plane. We taxied down the dusty runway and took off, flying low over the reef. I was sorry to leave Rodrigues; for from what I had seen of it, it seemed an enchanting and unspoiled island. I hoped that it would long remain so, for once tourism discovered its whereabouts, it would suffer the same fate as has befallen so many beautiful places on earth.

When we got back to Mauritius, we drove the bats down to the aviaries at Black River, which Dave had prepared for their reception. They had travelled very well and they settled down, hanging from the wire top of the aviary, chittering gently to each other and displaying great interest in the wide variety of food which Dave had prepared for them. Flushed with success, we went back to the hotel, had baths and then went in to dinner. When it came to the sweet course, Horace asked me what I would like.

'Well, what have you got?' I enquired, determined not to be caught, as we had been with the lobsters.

'Some nice fruit, Sir,' he said.

I looked at him. He did not appear to be pulling my leg.

'What sort of fruit?' I asked.

'We've got some beautiful, ripe Jak fruit, Sir,' he said enthusiastically.

I had cheese.

CHAPTER FIVE

THE ENCHANTED WORLD

Outside the French windows that led from the sitting-room of the hotel suite lay a spacious and cool verandah. Step off this, and one walked twenty yards or so across coarse grass planted with tall casuarina trees that sighed like lovers in the wind, until one came to the wide, frost-white beach with its broken necklace of corals and coloured shells, lying wavering across the shoreline. In the distance lay the reef, white and thunderous with surf, and beyond it the royal blue of the Indian Ocean. Between the white beach, decorated with its biscuit-brittle graveyard of coral fragments, and the wide reef with its ever-changing flower bed of foam, lay the lagoon. Half a mile of butterfly-blue water, smooth as a saucer of milk, clear as a diamond, which hid an enchanted world like none other on earth.

Any naturalist who is lucky enough to travel, at certain moments has experienced a feeling of overwhelming exultation at the beauty and complexity of life, and a feeling of depression that there is so much to see, to observe, to learn, that one lifetime is an unfairly short span to be allotted for such a paradise of enigmas as the world is. You get it when, for the first time, you see the beauty, variety and exuberance of a tropical rain forest, with its cathedral maze of a thousand different trees, each bedecked with gardens of orchids, epiphytes, enmeshed in a web of creepers; an interlocking of so many species that you cannot believe that number of different forms have evolved. You get it when you see for the first time a great concourse of mammals living together, or a vast, restless conglomeration of birds. You get it when you see a butterfly emerge from a chrysalis; a dragonfly from its pupa; when you observe the delicate, multifarious courtship displays, the rituals and taboos, that go into making up the continuation of a species. You get it when you first see a stick or a leaf turn into an insect, or a piece of dappled shade into a herd of zebras. You get it when you see a gigantic school of dolphins stretching as far as the eye can see, rocking and leaping exuberantly through their blue world; or a microscopic spider manufacturing from its frail body a transparent, apparently never-ending line that will act as a transport as it sets out on its aerial explorations of the vast world that surrounds it.

But there is one experience, perhaps above all others, that a naturalist should try to have before he dies, and that is the astonishing and humbling experience of exploring a tropical reef. It seems that in this one action you use nearly every one of your senses, and one feels that one could uncover hidden senses as well. You become a fish, hear, and see and feed as much like one as a human being can; yet at the same time you are like a bird, hovering, swooping and gliding across the marine pastures and forests.

I had obtained my first taste of this fabulous experience when I was on the Great Barrier Reef in Australia but there, unfortunately, we had only masks and no snorkels, and my mask let in water. To say that it was fascinating, was putting it mildly, for there below me was this fascinating, multi-coloured world and I could only obtain glimpses of it, the duration of which was dependent upon how long I could hold my breath and how long it took my mask to fill and drown me. The tantalising glimpses I *did* get of this underwater world were unforgettable and I determined to do it properly at the first available opportunity. This came in Mauritius, for there at the Le Morne Brabant Hotel, the lagoon and its attendant reef were literally on my doorstep. I could not have been closer without moving my bed into it.

The first morning, I made myself a pot of tea and carried it out on to the verandah, together with one of the small, sweet Mauritian pineapples. I sat eating and watching the boats arrive farther down the beach, each piloted by handsome, bright-eyed, long-haired fishermen ranging from copper-bronze to soot-black in colour, wearing a variety of clothing in eye-catching colours that shamed the hibiscus and bougainvillaea flowers that flamed in the gardens. Each boat was loaded down with a cargo of snow-white pieces of coral and multi-coloured, pard-spotted cowries and cone shells. From sticks stuck in the gunwales, hung necklaces of tiny shells like glittering rainbows. The sun had just emerged from the mountains behind the hotel. It turned the sky and the horizon powder-blue; gilded a few fat, white clouds that sailed in a slow flotilla across the sky; gave a crisp, white sparkle to the foam on the reef and turned the flat, still lagoon transparent sapphire.

Almost as soon as I had seated myself on the verandah, the table at which I sat had become covered with birds, anxious to share with me whatever breakfast I had. There were mynahs with neat, black and chocolate plumage and banana-yellow beaks and eyes; Singing finches, the females a delicate leaf-green and pale, butter-yellow, and the males, by contrast, strident sulphur-yellow and black; and the Whiskered bulbuls, black and white, with handsome scarlet whiskers and tail flash. They all had a drink out of the milk jug, decided the tea was too hot and then sat, looking longingly at my fruit. I extracted the last of the juicy core from the glyptodont skin of the pineapple and then placed the debris on the table where it immediately became invisible under a fluttering, bickering mass of birds.

I finished my tea and then, taking my mask and snorkel, made my way slowly down to the shore. I reached the sand and the ghost crabs (so transparent that when they stopped moving and froze, they disappeared) skittered across the tide ripples and dived for safety into their holes. At the rim of the lagoon, the sea lapped very gently at the white sand, like a kitten delicately lapping at a saucer of milk. I walked into the water up to my ankles and it was as warm as a tepid bath.

All round my feet on the surface of the sand were strange decorations that looked as though someone had walked through the shallow water and traced on the sandy bottom the blurred outlines of a hundred starfish. They lay arm to arm, as it were, like some strange, sandy constellation. The biggest measured a foot from arm tip to arm tip, and the smallest was about the size of a saucer.

Curious about these ghostly sand starfish, I dug an experimental toe under one and hooked upwards. It came out from under its covering and floated briefly upwards, shedding the film of sand that had been lightly covering it and revealing itself to be a fine, robust starfish of a pale brick-pink, heavily marked with a dull white and red speckling. Though they looked attractively soft and velvety – like a star you put on top of a Christmas tree – they were, in fact, hard and sandpaperish to the touch. The one I had so rudely jerked out of its sandy bed with my toe performed a languid cartwheel in the clear water and drifted down on to the bottom, landing on its back. Its underside was a pale, yellowish ivory, with a deep groove down each arm that looked like an open zip-fastener. Within this groove, lay its myriad feet – tiny tentacles some four millimetres long, ending in a plate-shaped sucker. Each foot could be used independently so that there was a constant movement in the grooves and the tentacles contracted and expanded, searching for some surface on which the suckers could fasten.

Discovering none, and presumably concluding that it was upside down, the starfish curled the extreme tip of one arm under itself. Finding a foothold, it then curled its arm further in an effortless, boneless sort of way. At the same time, it curled under the two arms on either side of the first one, and slowly and gently, the animal started to lift itself with this triangle of arms. The arms on the opposite side of its body curled and spread upwards like the fingers of a hand to support it, and soon the body was vertical like a wheel, supported by the ever-stiffening arms. The arms on the farthest side now spread wide and the body sank towards them slowly and gracefully like a yogi completing a complicated and beautiful asana. The body was now turned upright; it remained only for the starfish to pull out its remaining arms from underneath it and the animal was the right side up. The whole action had been performed with a slow-motion delicacy of movement that would have brought tears to the eyes of any ballet dancer.

Now, however, the starfish did something that no ballerina, be she ever too talented, could have emulated. It lay on the sand and simply disappeared. Before my eyes, it vanished and left behind it, like the Cheshire Cat left its smile, merely a vague outline, the suggestion of a starfish, as it were, embossed upon the sand. What had happened, of course, was that while the starfish remained apparently unmoving, its hundreds of little feet, out of sight beneath it, were burrowing into the sand, so the animal simply sank from view and the white grains drifted to cover it. The whole thing, from the moment I had unearthed the creature until it disappeared, had taken no longer than two minutes.

I had approached the lagoon with every intention of plunging in and swimming out to deep water, but I had already spent five minutes watching the ghost crabs, five minutes admiring the necklace of flotsam washed up by the tide, and another two minutes standing ankle-deep in the water watching what was obviously a guru starfish attaining a sort of sandy nirvana. During this time, the fishermen, perched like some gay parrots in their boats, had been regarding me with the same avid interest as I had bestowed upon the natural history of the shoreline. Their curiosity had been well concealed, however, and there had been no attempt to solicit my custom for their wares in the tiresome way that is indulged in by pedlars in other countries. Mauritians were too polite for that. I waved at them and they all waved back, grinning broadly.

Determined not to be sidetracked again, I waded out waist-deep into the water, put on my mask and plunged my head under the water to get my head and back wet and protect it a little from the sun, which was hot even at that early hour. As my mask dipped below the surface, the sea seemed to disappear and I was gazing down at my feet in the submarine territory that immediately surrounded them.

Instantly I forgot my firm resolve to swim out into deeper water, for I was surrounded by a world as bizarre as any science fiction writer had thought up for a Martian biology. Around my feet, a trifle close for comfort, lay six or seven large, flattish sea urchins, like a litter of hibernating hedgehogs with bits of seaweed and coral fragments enmeshed in their spines so that, until one looked closely, they appeared to be weed-covered lumps of dark lava. Entwined between them were several curious structures, lying on the sand in a languid manner, like sunbathing snakes. They were tubes some four feet long and about four inches in circumference. They looked like the submarine parts of a strange vacuum cleaner, apparently jointed every three inches and manufactured out of semi-opaque, damp brown paper that had started to grow a sort of furry fungus at intervals along its length.

At first, I could not believe that these weird objects were alive. I thought they must be strange, dead strands of some deep-sea seaweed now washed into the shallows by the tide, to roll and undulate helplessly on the sand to the small movements of the sea. Closer inspection showed me that they were indeed alive, unlikely though it seemed. *Sinucta muculata*, as this strange creature is called, is really a sort of elongated tube, which sucks in water at one end and with it microscopic organisms, and expels the water at the other.

As well as Sinucta, I saw some old friends lying about, placid on the sea-bed – the sea slug that I had known from my childhood in Greece, thick, fat, warty creatures, a foot long, looking like a particularly revolting form of liver sausage. I picked one up; it was faintly slimy, but firm to the touch, like decaying leather. I lifted it out of the water and it behaved exactly as its Mediterranean cousins did. It ejected a stream of water with considerable force, at the same time becoming limp and flaccid in my hand. Then, having exhausted this form of defence, it tried another one. It suddenly voided a stream of a white substance that looked like liquid latex and was sticky beyond belief, the slightest portion adhering to your skin more tenaciously than Sellotape.

I could not help feeling that this was a rather futile form of defence for should an enemy be attacking, this curtain of adhesive, rubber-like solution would only serve to bind it more closely to the sea slug. However, it seemed unlikely that any weapon as complex as this would have been evolved in a creature so primitive unless it had fulfilled a necessary purpose. I released the slug and he floated to the bottom, to roll gently on to the sand, fulfilling the gay, vibrant, experience-full life that sea slugs lead, which consists of sucking the water in at one end of their being and expelling it at the other, while being rolled endlessly by the tide.

Reluctantly, I dragged my attention away from the creatures that lived in the immediate vicinity of my feet, and launched myself on my voyage of exploration. That first moment, when you relax and float face downwards, and, under the glass of your mask, the water seems to disappear, is always startling and uncanny. You suddenly become a hawk, floating and soaring over the forests, mountains and sandy deserts of this marine universe. You feel like Icarus, as the sun warms your back, and below you, the multi-coloured world unfolds like a map. Though you may float only a few feet above the tapestry, the sounds come up to you muted as if floating up from a thousand feet in still air, as you might be suspended and hear sounds of life in the toy farms and villages below a mountain. The crunch of the gaudy parrot fish, rasping at the coral with its beak; the grunt or squeak or creakings of any one of a hundred fish, indignantly defending their territory against invaders; the gentle rustle of the sand moved by tides or currents; a whisper like the feminine rustle of a thousand crinolines. These and many more noises drift up to you from the sea bed.

At first, the sandy bottom was flat, littered with the debris of past storms and hurricanes; lumps of coral now covered with weed, and the abode of a million creatures; pieces of pumice stone. On the sand, lay battalions of huge, black sea urchins, with long, slender spines that move constantly like compass needles. Touch one of them, and the spines moving gently to and fro suddenly become violently agitated, waving about with ever-increasing speed like mad knitting needles. They were very fragile as well as being sharp, so that if they penetrated your skin, they broke off. They also stained the immediate area of the puncture, as though you had been given a minute injection of Indian ink. Although they looked black, when the sunlight caught them, you found that they were a most beautiful royal blue with a green base to each spine. This species was fortunately flamboyant enough to be very obvious and, although some lay in crevices and under coral ledges, the majority lay on the sand, singly or in prickly groups, and were very apparent.

Interspersed with these were more of the elongated hosepipes and a further scattering of sea slugs. These, however, appeared to be of a different species. They were very large, some of them eighteen inches long and a mottled, yellowish-green. They also seemed much smoother and fatter than their black cousins, most of them being some four or five inches in diameter. I dived down to pick up one of these dim and unattractive creatures. As I was swimming to the surface with him, he first of all squirted water in the usual way and then, finding this did not make me relinquish my grip on his fat body, exuded his sticky rubber.

I was astonished at the attractive effect it had under water. When the sea slug used this, his ultimate deterrent, in the air, it came out simply as a sort of squishy, white, sticky stream, but viewed under water, the same phenomenon was different and beautiful. The substance was revealed as being composed of fifty or more separate strands, each the thickness of fine spaghetti and about eight inches long. One end remained attached to the beast while the filaments at the other end curved out and floated in the water like a delicate white fountain. Whether these strands had the power to sting and perhaps paralyse small fish, I don't know. One could touch them without feeling anything or getting any irritation, but certainly, spread out in a graceful spray, the tentacles presented much more of an adhesive hazard to an enemy than I had thought.

I swam on and, quite suddenly, like a conjuring trick, I found I was swimming through and over a large school of extraordinary-looking fish. There were about fifty of them; each measured some three to four feet long and was coloured a neutrally-transparent grey, so that it was almost invisible. Their mouths protruded almost into an elongated spike, as did their tails, so that it was difficult to tell at first glance which way they were pointing until you saw their round, rather oafish eyes staring at you with caution. They had obviously been doing something very strenuous and were now exhausted. They hung, immobile in the water, facing the current, meditating. They were most orderly, for they hung in the water in ranks, like well-drilled, if somewhat emaciated soldiers. It was interesting to note that they hung in exactly the right juxtaposition to each other, like troops on parade, so many feet between the fish in front and behind, and the same distance between the one above and the one below and the ones on each side. My sudden presence caused a certain amount of panic in their ranks, like someone marching out of step on an Armistice Day parade, and they swam off in confusion. As soon as they put enough distance between themselves and me, they re-formed ranks, turned to face the tide, and went into a trance again.

Leaving these fish, I swam on, gazing enthralled at the sandy bottom, barred with broad stripes of gold by the sun and these, by some optical alchemy, spangled all over with golden, trembling rings. Then, looming up ahead of me, I saw a shape, a dim blur which materialised into a massive rock some nine feet by three, shaped like the dome of St Paul's Cathedral. As I got closer, I saw that the whole rock was encrusted with pink, white and greenish corals and on top of it there were four huge, pale bronze sea anemones, attached like flowers to a monstrous, multi-coloured bonnet.

I swam over this fascinating rock and anchored myself against the slow pull of the tide by catching hold of a projecting piece of coral, having first examined it care-fully to make sure that there was nothing harmful lurking on, or under, or in it. That this was a wise precaution, I soon realised for as soon as my eyes got focused, I saw lurking, almost invisible, in the coral-and reed-encrusted grotto, a foot or so away from my hand, a large and beautifully coloured Scorpion fish whose dorsal spines can cause you agony and even, in rare cases, death, should you unwittingly touch it and it jabs them into you. He was some seven inches long, with a jowly, pouting face and huge, scarlet eyes. His predominant colours were pink and orange, with black bars and stripes and specklings. His pectoral fins were greatly elongated so he looked as though he had two pink hands growing out from under his gills, with attenuated fingers. Along his back was the row of scarlet spines that could prove so lethal. Altogether, he was a most flamboyant fish and, once you had spotted him, he glowed like a great jewel; yet until I had noticed a slight movement from him, he had, with his striped and spotted livery, melted into the background. Now, realising he had been spotted, he moved his great trailing fins gently and gradually edged his way round and down the rock away from me. Beautiful though he was, I was relieved not to have him at quite such close quarters.

Living in and around the anemones, were some handsome Clown fish, about three inches long, a bright orange colour, banded with broad stripes of snow-white. These pretty little fish have a symbiotic relationship with the anemones. They live among the stinging tentacles which would kill other fish, and so the anemone becomes their home; a formidable fortress in which the Clown fish takes refuge in moments of danger. In return for this protection, the fish, of course, drops some of its food which then becomes the anemone's lunch. Why, or how, this curious relationship came about, is a mystery. Anemones can hardly be described as having scintillating intellects, and how they managed to work out the usefulness of the Clown fish and refrain from stinging them, is a puzzle.

Wedged deep into the coral here and there were a number of large clams. All that could be seen of them were the rims of their scalloped shells, over which the edge of their mantle protruded, so they appeared to be grinning at you with thick, blue and iridescent green lips. These, each about the size of a coconut, were, of course, relatives of the famous giant clam found farther out on the reef – a monstrous shell that could weigh up to two hundred pounds and measure three feet. Many blood-curdling stories have been written about unfortunate divers who by chance have put their foot into one of these shells, which immediately slammed shut like a man-trap (as all clams do in moments of stress) thus consigning the diver to death by drowning. There does not appear to be an authenticated record of this ever having happened, although of course it is perfectly possible, for the shell could snap shut and unless the diver had a knife with which to cut the massive muscle that acts as both hinge and lock on the two halves of the shell, it would be as immovable and unopenable as a castle door. Again, in the case of these highly coloured clams, there is a curious symbiotic relationship, for in the brilliant mantle there are a number of small, unicellular algae, called by the rather attractive name of

Zooxanthelae. These minute creatures obtain their sustenance from the food the clam sucks in, and in payment they give the clam an additional supply of oxygen. It is rather like paying for your daily bread with air, a thing most of us would like to do.

I shifted my vantage point to the other side of the rock, making sure of the whereabouts of the Scorpion fish, and came upon yet another symbiotic relationship. There was a small shoal of various multi-coloured fish, which included a Box fish and three canary-yellow Surgeon fish. The Box fish was quite incredible. He was only three inches long, vivid orange with black polka-dots all over him; but it was not the colouration so much as the bizarre shape of the creature which amazed me, for the whole body is like a square box of bone and through holes in this protrude the creature's fins, vent, eyes and mouth. This means that the tail has to wave around like the propeller of an outboard engine. This mode of locomotion, coupled with the fish's big, round, perpetually surprising-looking pop-eyes, its square shape and polka-dot suiting, combine to make it one of the most curious inhabitants of the reef.

The Surgeon fish were quite different. Their yellow bodies were roughly moon-shaped, they had high domed foreheads and their mouths protruded, almost like the snout of a pig. They get their name from the two sharp, scalpel-like knives set just behind the tail. These dangerous weapons can fold back like the blade of a pocket knife into a hidden groove.

But, fascinating though these two species of fish were, it was what was happening to them that was so curious. The two Surgeon fish were close to the rock, hanging in a trance-like state while the Box fish puttered to and fro like some weird, orange boat, occasionally coming to a standstill. Among them darted three lithe little fish, small gobies with bright Prussian-blue and sky-blue markings. They were cleaner fish and they worked assiduously on their three customers, zooming in to suck the parasites off their skin and then, as it were, standing back to admire their handiwork before dashing in again, rather like effeminate hairdressers admiring the creation of a new hairstyle. Later on, on the big main reef, I sometimes saw queues of fish waiting their turn at the barber's shop, where the little blue barbers worked in a frenzy to keep up with their customers.

So captivated had I become by all I had seen, for every inch of what we came affectionately to call 'St Paul's' was covered with tiny anemones, sea fans, feather worms, shrimps, crabs and a host of other things, that I discovered I had spent over an hour suspended in one spot and even then, had been unable to take it all in. Here, on this one rock, was a myriad of life which would require a naturalist to spend a dozen lifetimes even to start to unravel it. What, I wondered, as I swam slowly back to breakfast, was the reef going to be like? I was soon to know. It was overwhelming.

As soon as we could, I made arrangements for a boat and a boatman to come early each morning so that we would be able to spend a couple of hours on the reef without it interfering with our other activities. So, two days later, the boat puttered its way across the silk-smooth lagoon and ground, with a faint sigh, in the sand just outside our bedrooms. Abel entered our lives. He was a slender young Creole with extensive side whiskers and a moustache, a wide, engaging African grin and a curiously husky, high-pitched voice. He had been stricken with polio at 12 years old when Mauritius had a virulent epidemic of this frightful disease but though this had partially withered his right arm and leg, he was still agile in his boat and could swim and dive like a fish. Like most countrymen and fishermen, he was extraordinarily knowledgeable about the sea life and where to find it, but his learning was mixed up with much inaccurate folk lore. Nevertheless, his knowledge of the reef was superb and he could take you to see anything you asked him, from octopus to oysters; from long, pointed shells like unicorns' horns, spattered with blood-red spots, to coral forests that defy description.

The first day we went out with him, he explained that the reef was divided roughly into five sections. There was the deep water reef where you swam outside the lagoon; there was the sandy area with only a scattering of rocks (like 'St Paul's') along the shoreline; and then there were the three separate sections of coral bed. In each one you saw something different. So, the first day he took us out to what we called the 'Stags' Graveyard' or 'Landseer's Corner'.

First, we crossed the sandy stretch. Lying on the tiny deck in the bows, with the early morning sun warming my back, I could gaze down into the clear water. First there were a host of sea slugs and the strange hosepipe-like Sinucta, then literally thousands of the big, red starfish, lying ghost-like, just buried under the sand, and interspersed with these on top of the sand, a great many cushion starfish. These are fat and round, like a pudding, and the arms are short and blunt so that the edges look almost scalloped. They are a yellowy-orange in colour and studded all over with slimy, jet-black, conical spikes like straight rose thorns.

Gradually we passed over more and more crops of coral and then the sand disappeared and we were gliding over a multi-coloured Persian carpet of weed and coral, and schools of bright fish shot from under our bows. Reaching the spot he had chosen, Abel turned off his engine and tossed the anchor, a huge lump of iron with a ring on it, over the side. We came to a standstill in some six foot of water, so clear it would have made vodka look murky. Hastily, we donned our masks and slipped over the side of the boat into a world so enchanted that it surpassed all poetic descriptions of fairy land one had ever read or imagined. One's first impression was of a blaze of colour, gold, purple, green, orange, red, and every conceivable shade in between. Once you had got over your astonishment at this polychromatic world, it was the shapes that captured your imagination. In this particular section, the predominant coral was Stag's horn, exactly like a great graveyard of all the finest Victorian deer trophies, decked out in white and electric blue. Some were only a few feet high, but here and there the coral formed huge shapes like white and blue Christmas trees, through whose branches drifted flocks of small, multi-coloured fish, as parakeets drift and swoop through trees in a tropical forest. Interspersed with these forests of Stag's horn were the Brain corals, some as big as plum pudding, others the size of an armchair, and interspersed between these, a bewildering array of delicate sea fans, soft corals and weeds.

If their habitat was breathtaking and confusing by its diverse colouration and shape, then so were the inhabitants. I was interested in a certain similarity to the land. The small, multi-coloured fish flew through the forests of Stag's horn like flocks of birds while below, the black and white Damsel fish in schools moved like herds of zebra among the sea fans. From the crevices in the coral, another dark chocolate and pink-coloured fish with large fins and a sulky, pouting mouth came out to threaten you when you invaded its territory, spreading its fins as an elephant spreads its ears when it charges. Then there were smouldering orange and black fish, like tigers, prowling in the shadowy depths of coral and quick-moving flocks of slender orange-brown fish like gazelles or antelope. Here in crevices, like sleeping porcupines, lay sea urchins, vivid blue and jade-green, and others of palest lavender.

I swam through this enchanted world, drugged by the colours and bizarre shapes, until I rounded a coppice of Stag's horn with vivid blue tips to each spike, and came on a small, sandy clearing, with sea slugs and purple and black sea urchins littering the bottom. Over them lay in the water perhaps fifty or so small fish which were to become my favourites. They were about four inches long and at first glance, because of their position, they seemed to be all pale leaf-green, the tender and beautiful green of lime trees with their buds just about to burst but with an iridescence as if each fish had been varnished. As I swam closer, however, I discovered the most spectacular thing about them. Slightly wary of my proximity, they swam past me. As I followed them, they turned, in one blink of the eye, from their delicate leaf-green to the most beautiful blue, the blue they used to use in medieval paintings for the robes of the Virgin Mary, a Madonna blue, with the same iridescence.

Enchanted, I made haste to swim past them and then turn back again, and so in a flash they turned back once more to green. So beautiful was this effect that I spent half an hour harrying the poor school so that they turned now this way and now that, changing from green to blue and back to green again as the sunlight caught them. What was so astounding was that, as they all turned at the same moment, each fish changed instantly with its neighbour. Eventually, bored with my attention, they swam off determinedly into the forest of Stag's horn where I could not follow them at speed, and so I soon lost them; but for me, they had become one of the most beautiful fish of the reef. All the others – purple, yellow, bronze, wine-red; spotted, striped, sequined; of bizarre shapes and sizes – were fascinating but my Leaf fish as I call them, as they have no common name and rejoiced only in the scientific *Cromiis selurialis*, became, for me, the personification of the reef.

Abel was not taciturn, indeed he could be very loquacious if he thought the occasion warranted it, but if he thought your observations or instructions were of an imbecile nature, he would not reply.

'Abel,' you would say, sternly, 'we only want to go a short way today.'

Abel would be riveted by something in the blue distance, or maybe fall into a trance.

'Only a short way. We must be back by eight-thirty,' you would say.

Abel would look at you, unseeingly.

'Did you hear?' you would shout above the stutter of the engine.

His eyes, expressionless, would flick on to you briefly and then go back to their contemplation of the horizon. You would get back to the hotel by half past nine, owing Abel twice what you intended, but it was always worth every penny. He knew what you wanted and you did not.

Once we had been several times to taste the pleasures of the Stag's horn area, Abel, without any reference to us, took us to an area which we eventually named the 'crockery shop'. We dropped over the side expecting the prickly 'Swiss forest' of the Stag's horn, and were amazed at what we found. Here, the coral was in great plates or bowl shapes and was brown and with perforations like a brandy snap. In places, it was in tottering piles like a giant's washing-up, and in other places, it had formed monstrous candelabra or the sort of rococo fountains that you find in the beautiful gardens of remote French chateaux or Italian villas. This was totally unlike the Stag's horn forest, where you could swim *with* the fish, for here, if you got too close, they simply disappeared amongst the crockery, where you could not follow them. You had to adopt a new technique. You simply drifted slowly along and let the fish come to you.

It was here that I saw my first Moorish idol, one of the strangest-looking of fish. If you could imagine a delta-winged aircraft with wings curved into a point, a small, blunt tail and a very protuberant engine, the whole thing flying on its side and striped in yellow and white, and black, you would have some conception of this strange fish.

It was in the crockery shop too, that I was engulfed suddenly by a large school of coral-pink and orange fish, some eight to ten inches long and with enormous dark eyes. I had been floating there, watching a sea slug standing up on end and wondering what it was doing, when I caught a flash of red out of the corner of the side windows of my mask, and the next minute this flock of colourful fish surrounded me, swimming very languidly and coming close enough for me to touch, gazing at me with their soulful black eyes. I recognised them with delight as being a fish I had always wanted to meet, which rejoices in the name of the Wistful Squirrel fish. They certainly look wistful. They gazed at me with a sort of lugubrious expression that gave the impression that they had all just returned from an exceptionally trying interview with their bank managers. Their eyes seemed to be full of tears and they looked so depressed that I longed to comfort them in some way. Hoping to relieve their gloom, I dived down and overturned a slab of dead coral lying on the bottom, thus unearthing a host of titbits in the shapes of shrimps, crabs, minute worms and diabolical-looking black starfish with their writhing, snake-like limbs covered in what looked like fur. Normally, fish delighted in this largesse, but the Wistful Squirrel fish merely gazed at me in a grief-stricken way, and quietly edged away. Obviously I was not sufficiently sympathetic.

One of the exhausting things about swimming on the reef was the bewildering number of life forms that surrounded you everywhere you looked. In the four-and-a-half months that we were in Mauritius, we went out on the reef nearly every day and on each occasion, we would all see at least four new species of fish that we had not identified before. However, I really began to despair when, towards the end of our stay, Abel took us to the area we came to call the 'flower garden'; for it was here, in an hour's swim, that I hit the mind-boggling, all-time record of seeing sixteen species of fish I had not seen before during four months of snorkelling!

The flower garden was a very shallow reef, mostly three to three-and-a-half feet with parts of it only just over a foot in depth, so that you had to search for a channel through the coral lest you scrape your chest or knees. In this shallow water, the colours seemed even brighter and there were species of coral which one did not find elsewhere – the Mushroom coral, for example, which is free-living; that is to say, it does not form a reef as the other corals do, but lies about on the bottom, moving from place to place. It looks like the underside of a large, pinky-red and brown mushroom and only when the small, pale yellow tentacles come out from between the gills and wave about, do you realise that it is alive. Then there were the corals that looked like mounds of tiny green chrysanthemums, the size of a little finger nail. These were in constant movement and so they looked like great mounds of flowers being blown by some underwater breeze. And there were the startlingly vivid blue corals, a really bright cobalt blue; and the red corals which varied from the colour of blood to the palest sunset-pink. One could see heads of coral that looked as though they had been neatly clipped into round shapes by an expert in topiary. Each of these heads was so neat that you could not believe they had grown like that. Closer inspection revealed that each of these heads (about the size of a large bouquet of flowers) consisted of pieces of coral shaped like small, snow-covered Christmas trees.

It was these coral heads that were particularly favoured by the Leaf fish, which would float in schools near them and take refuge from danger by diving in amongst the Christmas trees. It was near one of these corals that I found a school of about fifty baby Leaf fish. At that age, I discovered, they do not possess the green iridescence but are sky blue, a much lighter shade than the adults, but just as exquisite. I amused myself for a long time by simply stretching out my hand towards this glittering group of minute fish, whereupon they would dive into the coral and disappear. The moment my hand was withdrawn, they would reappear out of the coral head like blue confetti bursting from a snow-covered pine forest.

It was in the flower garden that you saw the greatest number of species in the smallest area, and it was particularly attractive because, owing to the shallow water, you could get closer to them. The File fish were always a joy to watch. These were leaf-shaped fish with a curved, unicorn's horn on their foreheads, a brilliant green with longitudinal lines and bright orange spots, an orange striped snout and orange and black striped eyes. They get their name from the rough file-like quality of their skins. A relative of the File fish is the Trigger fish which goes locally by the jaw-breaking name of Humu-humu-nuku-nuku-a-puaa. They are a deep-bodied fish, roughly leaf-shaped but instead of having a protracted mouth like the File fish, the Trigger fish has a pouting, belligerent face like a Brigadier-General watching slovenly recruits. This is helped by its striped uniform of black and white and grey, and a bright blue band across the top of its nose, which makes it look as though it has got bushy eyebrows. The Trigger fish gets its name from a rather extraordinary defence mechanism. Like the File fish, it has a sort of curved horn, but this lies behind the eyes and can lie flat. When the fish is pursued by an enemy, however, this spine erects and another, smaller spine locks it into position to keep the trigger erect and immovable. This not only makes the fish a difficult and dangerous mouthful, but when it dives into the coral and erects its trigger, it is impossible to dislodge it without dismantling the whole coral head.

It was in this area that an incident happened that took me back to my childhood in Greece, when I used to go out with the fishermen. I was swimming down a canyon between the multi-coloured pieces of coral, when I came to an open, sandy area where I arrived simultaneously with an octopus, with tentacles some four feet long, who had just decided to shift from one area of the reef to another. When he saw me, he increased speed across the sand, looking unpleasantly like a hunchback with a trailing cloak of tentacles. He could not make it to the reef proper, so he took refuge in a large coral head in the middle of a sandy area. I swam over to see what he was up to, and found that he had wedged himself, or rather squished himself, into a small crevice and had slitted his eyes, as octopus do when in danger, for the eyes are very obvious otherwise. His skin was flashing and blushing, as octopus always do in moments of stress, in a startling variety of colours, including peacock blues and greens. Instead of making him more obvious, this firework display of colours helped him to merge in with his colourful background. I was within three or four feet of him, wondering if I could flush him out, when a trident slid down over my shoulder and plunged into the octopus, which immediately became a writhing, Medusa head of tentacles. Great gouts of black ink stained the water as Abel, who had manoeuvred the boat up behind me, triumphantly hauled the wriggling octopus on board.

Having a dying octopus spouting ink pulled up nearly into my face was not the pleasantest memory I had of the reef, which is a ravishing place, indescribably beautiful and complex. At present, it is exploited and over-fished; shells are collected for sale and the coral is dynamited so that bits may be carried home by triumphant tourists, pathetic pieces of once-beautiful living organisms to collect dust on some distant mantelpiece. It is to be hoped that the Mauritian Government will follow the enlightened lead of other Governments, such as those of the Seychelles and Tanzania, and declare its reefs Marine National Parks so that their beauty may be a joy for ever to visitors and to Mauritians alike; for the reef is an elixir that is within reach of all.

As I write this, the sky outside is grey and a fine snow is falling, but I have only to close my eyes and I can recall the splendours of the reef and they warm and cheer me.

In the flower garden one day I suddenly came upon a huge concourse of Leaf fish. There must have been a couple of thousand of them, spread over an area of fifty or sixty square feet. I swam with them for half an hour and it was unforgettable; one moment it was like being in a forest of green leaves greeting the spring, the next like floating through bits of Mediterranean-blue sky that had miraculously fallen into the sea in the shape of fish. At length, drugged and dazzled, I found a smooth coral head free from urchins and Scorpion fish and sat on it in two feet of water. I took off my mask and there, in the distance, were the mountains of Mauritius humped and shouldering their way to the horizon, like uneasy limbs under a bed covering of green forest and patchwork quilt of sugar cane with here an elbow and there a knee of hill sticking up. Across this were looped no less than five rainbows. I decided I liked Mauritius very much indeed.

CHAPTER SIX

BOA-HUNT

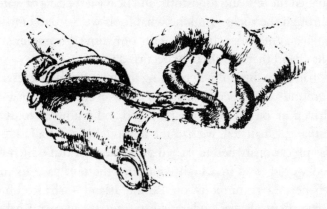

The boat thrust its way across the blue hummocks of waves and against the yellow and green dawn sky the carapace of Round Island loomed up, grim and forbidding.

A year had passed and we had come this time for four days, so we were well equipped for that most inhospitable spot. As well as the normal camping equipment, we had jerry cans of precious water and plenty of food. On an island where you might be trapped by sudden bad weather, it was essential that you took enough food and water to provide for this eventuality. However, the sheer weight and quantity of our supplies dictated that our camp should be somewhat near the landing rock, far enough away as to avoid heavy seas but not so far that it was impossible to lug our equipment there.

The weather was kind to us and the landing of our supplies and equipment was not as hazardous as it might have been, but the transporting of the stuff two or three hundred feet to the cleft in the rocks we had chosen for a camp site proved very exhausting, even though the sun was only just above the horizon well hidden by the island's bulk. Cursing and sweating, we lugged the tent and foodstuffs, and heavy jerry cans of water, up through the rocks, thinking what fools we were to embark on such an enterprise. It was not the only time during our stay on the island that this thought occurred to us.

We had great difficulty in pitching the tent, for in that terrain the ground was either too hard to allow even a steel spike to be driven in, or else the tuff splintered and crumbled to dust. Eventually, exhausted, we had the tent pitched after a fashion. It was precariously tied to jagged projections of tuff which we hoped would hold in a high wind, but the tent gave us that much-needed commodity on Round Island – shade. Until one has spent all day under a blistering sun in a sun-baked terrain, one does not appreciate that even the shade cast by a toy umbrella can be as welcome as a deep, cool cave. Nor does one realise that even hot water to drink is better than no water at all.

Having seen us safely installed and made sure that we knew how to use the portable radio – our only link with the outside world – Wahab went back to the good ship *Sphyrna* which means Hammer-head shark. Soon they were a mere speck against the sea, heading far past Gunner's Quoin along towards the blurred, blue, distant mountains of Mauritius. By the time we had finished rearranging the jerry cans, to our surprise we were very tired and so, after a meagre supper, for the heat, we found, took our appetite away, we went to bed just after sunset.

Next morning, we were up before dawn and made our way up to the old Screw pine or vacoa, known as the picnic tree, since it is the first shade-giving tree of consequence you come to on your climb up from the landing stage, and so it is there that everyone picnics. From here, we decided to make our way in a straight line, or as straight a line as is possible on Round Island, through the palm belt, northwards. We would work fifty feet or so apart, zig-zagging from Latania palm to Latania palm, in which, reputedly, the boas lived, and make a thorough search of each one. When it got too hot, we intended to drop down fifty feet and make our way back to camp. By this means, we hoped to have examined every likely palm in a hundred-foot strip for about half a mile's length. To anyone who does not think this sounds like a very arduous undertaking, may I suggest they go out to Round Island and try it.

For the first hour, we searched assiduously. We were constantly having false alarms when we found placid and friendly Telfair's skinks or bushbaby-eyed Gunther's geckos in the axil of the palm leaves – a skink or gecko's tail, when that is all you can see, looks very like a snake at first glance. It was nice to notice, however, that the Telfair's population had increased by leaps and bounds since the previous year and, more important, the Gunther's gecko population had increased as well. Everywhere there were fat babies in evidence.

We understood from everyone who had seen or captured one of the boas that the commoner of the two species – if you can call an estimated population of seventy-five common – could be found lurking in the axil of the leaves of the Latania palm. To those who had never seen a Latania, these seemed concise, straight-forward instructions, nothing could have been simpler. The Latanias, however, make life very difficult. The fronds grow on a thick, straight stalk that ends in something like a giant green fan. The stalk has all the resilience of cast iron and the fan part appears to be manufactured out of thick and indestructible green plastic. The tip of the fan is armed with tiny spikes, sharp enough to put out one's eye. So looking for the Round Island boa, one had to approach a Latania, part the fronds and push one's face into the interior of the palm until one could see the axils of the leaves, exerting considerable pressure on the leaves and hoping meanwhile that the stalk did not slip through one's sweaty hand and allow the fan to lacerate or blind one.

The other species, the Burrowing boa, is fossorial and to find this one had to dig hopefully, like a pig in an oak wood, into the shallow area of earth trapped round the base of each palm. On the face of it, this too should have proved easy but it was not, for the dead leaves of the Latania, though they turned brown and fell earthwards, still remained attached by their stalks to the parent tree; thus they formed a sort of resilient brown tent of fan-shaped leaves round the base of each tree, and these had to be moved aside before one could grub in the earth they concealed. To say that this was thirst- and sweat-provoking work was an understatement; you were bathed in perspiration and yet your body glowed with heat, and your tongue appeared to have taken up residence in a cave composed of very old and very dry chamois leather. The tuff grew so hot that you could have coddled an egg on it. From above, the heat hit you like a physical blow, while it rebounded from the tuff, and hit you in the face with a blast like opening a foundry oven. We lost more moisture in sweat walking a hundred yards than one would have thought the body could contain.

The exhausting part was that you were never on the level. Either you were straining your muscles to climb uphill, or straining them against the downward slope. Even when you walked in a straight line, you felt you were walking with one leg shorter than the other. We searched for two hours and then sat down to have a much-needed drink and an orange apiece. We found, as we got more used to hunting on Round Island, that oranges were better value to take with you than the heavy bottles of water, for they provided you with moisture as well as food, and left your clogged mouth feeling clean.

By now, the sun had crept up and peered over the carapace of the island, glowering down at us like the monstrous red-hot eye of some giant dragon. We knew that it would soon be really too hot to continue our search. We moved downhill some fifty feet and started back to camp, searching as we went. I parted the leaves of a Latania for what seemed like the thousandth time, and saw the tail of what I thought was a Telfair's skink. I was about to move along to the next palm, when I thought I had better make sure it was a Telfair's. I had a brief struggle with the leaves and shifted my vantage point.

It was not a Telfair's but a fully-grown and very beautiful Round Island boa, which lay coiled around the Latania stems where the bases formed a sort of cup round the palm's trunk. From my viewpoint, I could see him lying there, languid and unafraid. The only portion of him I could catch hold of was the extreme end of his tail. This struck me as being a bad policy from every point of view. For one thing the tail was slender and, although unlikely to snap, could bruise more easily than the rest of his length. For another, if I grabbed him by the tail, he might bite me. This was no problem as far as I was concerned, as his mouth was tiny, but I did not want to risk breaking off some of his fish-bone-like teeth in my hand, which could then easily lead to his getting canker of the mouth. He was too valuable to risk anything like that. So, rather than move my position and risk disturbing him and maybe losing my find I called John who was upside down, like a dabbling duck, in the depths of the Latania farther down the hill.

'John,' I shouted, 'I've got a snake here, come and give a hand.'

He emerged, scratched, tousled and perspiring, his spectacles misted over, from the depths of his palm. He wiped his brow.

'Sorry,' he said. 'I'm too busy with the one hundred and fifty I've got here.'

'Don't be a nincompoop,' I said. 'I'm not joking.'

'Seriously?' said John, and then he ran towards me, stumbling and slipping on the tuff, and arrived panting.

'Go round to the other side of the palm and grab him,' I instructed. 'That's where his head is. And don't let him bite you, I don't want him to get canker of the mouth.'

With me acting as the rear guard, John parted the fronds, found out where the snake's head was deployed, and then simply inserted a long arm, picked him up by the back of the neck, gently disentangled him from the Latania leaves, and drew him out.

He was about three feet long; basically a pale olive-green colour, with a speckling of dull yellow towards the tail. The head was long and narrow, almost leaf-shaped. Altogether, he did not look very boa-like.

To say that we were exuberant was an understatement. To have captured one of the rarest snakes in the world in such difficult terrain, after only a two-hour search, was incredible; to have captured it, as it were, with its full co-operation, was even more extraordinary. We went back to our hunting with redoubled zeal. However, the sun rose higher and higher, and grew hotter and hotter, and the Latanias seemed tougher and tougher to wrestle with, so eventually we went back to camp and the luxury of fresh coconut milk, water melon, and camp beds that bucked like unbroken horses on the uneven terrain. In what we referred to, with some sarcasm, as the cool of the evening, when the temperature had dropped to a mere 85°F and you could sit on the exposed tuff without burning yourself, we did another sweep through the Latanias, but with no success. That night, it rained and the water poured down the sheets of tuff and through our tent so that, lying in our camp beds, it felt as if one were afloat on one of the less salubrious canals of Venice.

We were up before sunrise and just as the sky was turning greeny gold, we made our first sweep through the palm belt. I was much cooler that morning, for there had been a stiff breeze blowing, flecking the blue sea with white petals of foam and drawing great, flat flotillas of cloud across the sky which frequently masked the sun and gave us a few minutes' respite. We searched for three hours but although we saw lots of lizards, there were no snakes. When we stopped for a rest and an orange, John expounded a theory.

'You know, there is plenty for them to eat,' he said.

'I've seen no end of green geckos and baby skinks, which make ideal food.'

'There is certainly no shortage of food,' I said.

'Well, why are they so rare?' persisted John.

'Probably because they find it so hard to find each other in these damn Latanias,' I said bitterly.

'I think it's because they are preyed upon when they are young.'

'Preyed upon? What by?'

'Telfair's skinks. I've been watching the big ones and you know they eat anything from chewing gum to orange peel. Well,

I saw a Telfair's just now, eating quite a large Bojeri skink. The snakes can't be all that big when they are born. A fully-grown Telfair's is a formidable beast, and they are everywhere.'

'You're probably right, it hadn't occurred to me.'

'In fact,' said John, 'to help the snake in its wild state, it might be necessary to catch up four or five hundred Telfair's and transport them to Gunner's Quoin or Flat Island.'

'Now you are going too far,' I said, hopefully burying my orange pips in some loose tuff. 'You know there are two things that make all conservationists as hysterical as maiden aunts when they are suggested. One is captive breeding and the other is translocation of species.'

'Well, I think it would help the boa,' said John, stubbornly.

'It probably would. When we get our teeth really stuck into the Round Island problem, we'll suggest it. Meanwhile, let's have another tilt at these Latanias.'

Half an hour later, John's theory had some evidence to strengthen it. He had called me over to help him with a group of Latanias which were growing tightly together and which he found he was unable to explore single-handed. While I held the fresh leaves back, he grubbed around at the base of the palm among the dead fronds. He uprooted one of these, over which the rains had plastered a layer of tuff, and, suddenly, out fell what at first sight I took to be a large centipede, which lay, writhing, on the ground. Next moment, I realised it was a bright brick-red and yellow baby snake, some twelve inches long and as thick as a pencil. It was its astonishing colour that had me think it was a centipede, for I was unprepared for the juvenile colouration being so very vivid in contrast to the sober adult. We gathered up the baby in triumph, placed it tenderly in a cloth bag, and stumbled back to camp with it.

'There you are,' panted John, as we slipped and slithered

over Round Island's back. 'This little chap would have been helpless against the big Telfairs's, and it would have just made a nice meal for one of them too.'

That night, it not only rained heavily but the wind blew so hard that we were in danger of losing the tent altogether. It was a most uncomfortable night, and we were glad when the dawn came. We did our normal, routine hunt through the Latanias and returned at eleven o'clock. The sea had become considerably rougher and the sky was clouded over. The wind was coming in sudden vehement gusts, and it looked as if we were in for more rain before the day was out. During the course of lunch, I happened to stick my head outside the tent when I saw, to my astonishment, the good ship *Sphyrna* gallantly ploughing her way towards us, making heavy weather, for the sea was now quite rough. We speculated on what curious mission she could be involved in such inclement weather; then it gradually became obvious that she was heading for Round Island. We wondered what vital supplies Wahab could be sending us. It never occurred to us that it might be the weather itself that was the reason for the boat's hasty visit. When she got close to the landing rock and had put her anchor down, the captain hailed us.

'Cyclone,' he shouted. 'Force two warning in Mauritius. I've come to take you back, you must hurry.'

The idea of being marooned for an indeterminate period on Round Island while it underwent a cyclone of whatever magnitude was so unappealing that we hardly needed the captain's exhortation to hurry. Never was a camp broken and packed with such speed. Getting everything into the boat and then from the boat into the *Sphyrna* was an extremely hazardous experience, but eventually we, our gear and our two precious snakes were being buffeted and tossed by the waves on our way to Mauritius.

The cyclone warning lasted for a week – a week of oppressive weather, rain and rough seas. To cap it all, I had started to feel unwell on Round Island and this now developed into one of those amoeboid infections, which are so irritating and debilitating. It seemed as though our chance of returning to the island to get the required number of snakes for our breeding programme was non-existent; and we had not even collected the other lizard we needed. This meant that we would have to leave the snakes with Wahab to be taken back to Round Island and released. They were far too rare to risk making a mistake with, and the youngster could not be sexed with certainty with the facilities we had in Mauritius. It would be criminal to take them back to Jersey only to find that both snakes were the same sex. I discussed this at length with Wahab, and he said that the long range forecast was that the cyclone was going to miss us after all, and we were moving into a period of smooth weather. 'Would it not be possible for you to stay a little longer?'

I had, to my intense annoyance, since it had taken over seven years to arrange, just had to cancel a trip to Assam, which I was to have undertaken immediately on my return to Jersey, since the doctors in Mauritius advised against it. This gave me a little lee-way but even if we stayed, I decided, I was feeling too lousy to undertake the boat trip and the subsequent humping of heavy equipment round the island.

'Could we,' I asked, hopefully, 'get the Government helicopter? First, it would make the whole journey there and back infinitely easier and, secondly, I have always longed to do a trip in a helicopter.'

Wahab pursed his lips and said it would be difficult, but he would try.

A few days later, with an air of smug satisfaction, he phoned me up to say that the Prime Minister had given permission for us to have the helicopter. We could go as soon as the weather was right. For several days, we had to hang about while two cyclones, one with the endearing name of 'Fifi', whirled about the Indian Ocean, making up their minds whether or not to pay Mauritius a visit. To our great relief, they decided not to, and the weather forecast being propitious, we got the all-clear to embark on the following Monday. As it coincided with a series of public holidays, Wahab decided to join us and bring with him a stalwart volunteer from the Forestry Department to help us in our task.

We were to pick up the helicopter in Port Louis and thence to fly to a football field in the north of the island, where the lorry, with our supplies, would meet us. From there, it was only a quarter of an hour's flight to Round Island. We duly assembled at the Police Barracks in Port Louis and, with much solemnity, the helicopter was wheeled out and opened up like a bubble car. We clambered in. Wahab and John sat behind, while I was in front with the jovial Indian pilot and his co-pilot. It was, I decided, rather like being in a goldfish bowl and, having no head for heights, I wondered what it was going to feel like when we took off.

'My God, what a hot today,' said the pilot, fastening his seat belt and giving a fair imitation of Peter Sellers. 'What a bloody hot.'

'It will be hotter on Round Island,' I said.

'Yes, my God,' said the pilot, 'there you will be roasting. What a hot.'

The propeller whirled round faster and faster, and suddenly we rose vertically like a lift, remained stationary for a moment and then zoomed off seventy feet above the roofs of Port Louis. The sensation was incredible; one realised, much more vividly even than in a small plane, what it was like to be a hawk or dragonfly, to be able to rise and descend vertically, to hover and swoop. As we sped one hundred feet above the squares of sugar cane, each with its central pile of huge, brown rocks that had been ploughed up, one had the impression that one was flying over a vast, green chess board, covered with monstrous elephant droppings. Along the road, the Flamboyant trees glowed like heaps of live coals, and the roads themselves were dotted, like an Impressionist painting, with little specks of colour, which were the women, in their multi-coloured saris, going to market.

Presently we banked steeply – a not altogether pleasant sensation in a goldfish bowl, for you felt you were bound to crash through the glass and fall out – and came in to land on the football pitch, as lightly as a dandelion clock. Here, the lorry, piled high with our tent, foodstuffs and sixteen huge jerry cans of water, was waiting for us, accompanied by Wahab's side-kick from the Forestry Department, a young man called Zozo. He was a slender youth of Asian descent, with a wide and engaging grin, and a nose so retroussé that facing him was like looking up the barrels of a shotgun. His clothes were khaki drill, and he was wearing a huge pair of sunglasses and a large khaki solar topee – Forestry Department issue – of the type that used to be favoured by Stanley and Livingstone. He seemed an enchanting young man, terribly excited at the adventure. He confided to me that not only had he never left Mauritius before, but that he had never flown before, still less flown in a helicopter. To have three such extraordinary things happen in one day rendered him almost speechless.

We loaded our stuff into the helicopter, which had to make two trips because of the weight of the water, and took off. We swept low over the goalposts and the crowd of children, assembled to watch us, scattered and ran, laughing and screaming. Then

we roared up over the shaggy-headed palms and zoomed out over the emerald waters of the lagoon, over the foam flower bed of the reef, and then across the deep blue waters towards Round Island, that crouched, like a desiccated green and brown tortoise, on the horizon, fourteen miles away.

On the maps of Round Island, there are two areas in the south, marked 'Big Helipad' and 'Small Helipad'. With these grandiose titles, you might imagine a smooth area of tarmac, wind socks, perhaps, and even a Customs and Immigration shed and a Tourist Bureau. Fortunately no such amenities exist. The helipads are simply two flattened areas, one larger than the other, which are, indeed, the only flattened areas of any size on the island. Here, the wind and the rain had beaten, broken and smoothed the tuff into patches which, if not exactly smooth as a ballroom, were a reasonably level sort of moonscape. We landed on the smaller one, the whirling of our propellers sending the White- and Red-tailed tropic birds and the dark, rather sinister, Trinidad petrels, whirling and calling around us. The petrels had the most peculiar and ethereal cry, that started off with a series of croaks and ended with a bubbling song of great beauty and wildness, not the sort of noise you would expect from a drab seabird. In contrast, the fairy-like beauty of the tropic birds did not lead you to expect a noise like somebody having difficulty in getting a champagne cork out of a bottle.

Struggling and sweating, we manhandled our tent and supplies across the helipad and down the valley that ran alongside it, while the tropic birds dive-bombed us like white icicles, creaking their strange cries, and the petrels, effortlessly gliding two feet above the ground, accompanied us like highly polished sheep dogs guarding a flock of unruly and irresponsible sheep.

The camp site we chose was on the banks of the eroded, wind- and water-sculptured gully which ran, like a miniature Grand Canyon, towards the sea. Here, the tuff lay in great, grey sheets and between these, there were areas where it had been scratched and powdered into a form of soil by a combination of rabbits and seabirds. Over this grew a green layer of small, fleshy-stemmed plants which, at first glance, looked not unlike watercress. Fortunately it was not eaten by the rabbits, so it formed a protective covering for those precious areas of soil. The patches looked like a series of incongruous green meadows with a scattering of palms in the harsh, eroded landscape. They seemed innocent enough and devoid of life, except for insects and a few prowling skinks, but as soon as darkness fell, the whole picture changed.

It took us until dark to get the camp set up and functioning properly. As the green twilight faded and the sky turned velvety black, awash with stars, as if at a given signal there arose the most extraordinary noise from the bowels of the earth. It started softly, almost tunefully, a sound like a distant pack of wolves, howling mournfully across some remote, snowbound landscape. Then, as more and more voices joined the chorus, it became a gigantic, mad mass being celebrated underground in some Bedlamite cathedral. You could hear the lunatic cries of the priests and the wild responses from the congregation. This lasted for about half an hour, the sounds rising and falling, the ground throbbing with the noise, and then, as suddenly as if the earth had burst open and released all the damned souls from some Gustave Doré subterranean hell, out of the holes concealed by the green meadows, mewing and honking and moaning, the baby Shearwaters burst forth.

They appeared in hundreds, as if newly arisen from the grave, and squatted and fluttered around our camp, providing such a cacophony of sound that we could hardly hear each other speak. Not content with this, the babies, being of limited intelligence, decided that our tent was a sort of superior nest burrow, designed for their special benefit. Squaking and moaning, they fought their way in through the openings and flapped over and under our camp beds, defecating with great freedom, and if handled without tact, regurgitating a fishy, smelly oil all over us.

'Really, this is too much,' I said, as I evicted the twentieth baby from my bed, 'I know I am supposed to be an animal lover, but there are limits.'

'We can lace up the ends of the tent, Gerry,' said Wahab, 'but it will be very hot.'

'Well, I think I'd rather suffocate than share my bed with this avian cohort. Already my bed looks as though it were one of the more productive guano islands of Peru,' I said bitterly, rescuing a baby Shearwater which had just fallen into my soup.

So we laced up the ends of the tent. Beyond sending the temperature up into the hundreds, this had little effect, for the babies, undaunted, started burrowing under the sides of the tent. Every time they successfully did this, we had to unlace the ends to throw them out. In the end, we had to lay our jerry cans of water along the edges of the tent to repel the determined invaders. Defeated at last, the babies sat outside the tent and gave us the benefit of their singing throughout the night.

'Waaah, waaah, wooo,' one crowd would shout, and the others would reply, 'Waaah, waaah, wooee,' while a rival group sang 'Ooo, ooh, ooh, OOOHH, ooh,' and were backed up by a chorus 'Waah, waah, waah, ooeeee, waah, waah.'

This lasted until dawn. The only thing to break the monotony was when the parent birds flew in with food, and the strange cries of the babies were interspersed with peculiar and not very attractive sounds like a bath, full of liquid manure, running out. This was the parent birds regurgitating semi-digested fish. The tent began to smell like the interior of a whaling ship after a rich haul.

Towards dawn, when, through sheer exhaustion, we were falling into a fitful sleep in spite of the noise, the babies discovered a new virtue of the tent. Its sides were designed with beautifully arranged canvas slopes. The baby birds took it in turn to fly up on to the ridge of the tent and then to slide down the side, their claws making a noise like ripping calico on the canvas, while their brethren sat in a circle round about and made admiring cries, such as 'Caaw, cooRR, COORR,' and 'Oooh, Coorr, Coorr.' On mature reflection, I decided that this was the most uncomfortable night I had ever spent in my life.

The following morning, just before dawn, we awoke from our inadequate doze and staggered out from the tent, tripping and

stumbling to have a wash through the hordes of Shearwaters which still sat, honking, outside their burrows. The sky was pink, orange and green, with a handful of dark clouds scattered carelessly along the horizon. The sea was calm, a deep, cobalt blue. Over my head, the palms rustled their leaves with a sound like spectral rain, their fronds stamped black against the sky. Resting among them in an abandoned position on her back, was a fragile sickle moon, white as a tropic bird. The sky was freckled with the shapes of Shearwaters, flying and calling in a dawn chorus, and everywhere the dusky babies shuffled through the tobacco plants and scuttled into their holes.

Having had breakfast, we set off to the palm belt and here, we instructed Zozo in the art of snake catching. He asked, with a fine insouciance, whether he was actually to catch the snakes or just to find them. We said it would be fine if he just found them. So, pushing his solar topee on to the back of his head, and settling his sunglasses more firmly on his Pekinese nose, he set off. Within half an hour, to our astonishment, he called out that he had found a snake. We bore down on the Latania by which he was standing. Secretly, I felt sure that what he had discovered would be the tail of a Telfair's skink, but there, in the leaves, lying placidly, without fear, was a semi-grown boa. It had a fine, slender head and its colouring – in contrast to the greenish shade of the adult and the vivid, fox-red and yellow of the baby – was dark olive with a lacy network of dull yellow patches on its neck, parts of its back and the base of its tail. We congratulated Zozo on his brilliance until his grin of delight almost encircled his head; and so we continued on our way, exhilarated that we had met with such success so swiftly.

During our search for snakes, we, of course, still pursued the Gunther's geckos for we wanted some more young females, as well as the Bojeri and Telfair's skinks. Zozo, flushed with enthusiasm at his prowess as a snake hunter, got so daring that he actually caught several of the agile, glittering Bojeri skinks and then confessed to me, having glanced round to make sure that he was not overheard, that before this expedition, he had actually been afraid of lizards. We searched on until the sun grew too hot for comfort, and then made our way back to camp. We were well satisfied, for we had eight Bojeri skinks, six young Telfair's skinks and three half-grown Gunther's geckos, as well as the snake. Later in the afternoon, when a little of the heat had gone out of the sun, we made another sortie through the Latania belt, but with no success. That night, we once again had a cacophonous company of the Shearwaters and slept fitfully.

Next morning, we decided to leave extra early, to make our way to one of the highest points of the island and then work downwards towards the sea. Climbing upwards, even that early in the morning, was an exhausting process and by the time we reached the highest vantage point, we were bathed in sweat.

Here one saw how eroded the island was, with the cliffsides of tuff falling sheer as a ski-slope down to the sea, grooved and veined into channels by the rain. Here and there lay boulders that had been unearthed from the tuff and tumbled into gullies in toppling piles, awaiting the next deluge to take them farther down towards their final resting place in the sea. At the summit the great sheets of tuff were hard enough, but we had had a little rain in the night and in places it had dissolved into something like the consistency of a slab of chocolate in a schoolboy's pocket, sticky, slippery and full of foreign bodies. On these slopes, you had to move with extreme care for if you lost your footing, you would roll unhindered three or four hundred feet, until you crashed into the palm belt, or else, if you fell in a gully, nothing would impede your descent until you hit the sea some seven hundred feet below.

Gazing down at these steep slopes of tuff gouged into massive wrinkles by the rain, with what palms there were leaning over precariously in their efforts to retain their grip, and below, a carpet of tuff silt lying on the bottom of the sea, you realised forcibly that here was a unique, miniature world that had, by a miracle of evolution, come into being and was now being allowed to bleed to death. The twisted sheets and shelves of tuff were being drained away, while over them sprawled the trailing, inadequate tourniquets of the convolvulus plants, with their purple funeral flowers. While everyone argued over what to do about the rabbits, and got no forrader, this unique speck of land was diminishing day by day. It seemed to sum up in miniature what we were doing to the whole planet, with millions of species being bled to death for want of a little, so little, medicare.

For an hour or so, we made our way slowly seawards, zig-zagging down the steep sides, investigating the little copses of Latanias that huddled grimly wherever they could get a roothold. Even at this height, I found that these miniature woodlands of palms contained a myriad of creatures. There were cockroaches and crickets; beetles, flies, a strange larva wearing a case that looked like an ice-cream cone; stick insects, spiders; and on every exposed area a billion tiny mites, scarlet as huntsmen, rushing, apparently aimlessly, about the tuff. In holes under the dead Latania leaves curious purple-coloured land crabs with pale, cream-coloured claws which they waved to and fro, looking like bank clerks who had spent their lives endlessly counting other people's money and now could not stop the reflex action of their hands. All around the Latanias lived the Telfair's skinks, and you only had to sit down for a minute for them to come clustering round you with the curiosity of children, trying to eat your shoe laces or your

trouser bottoms, and devouring everything else that you threw down, from orange peel to paper. Here, in the grassy areas around the Latanias, lived the Bojeri, moving like quicksilver in the sun on their perpetual hunt for food, and on the Latanias themselves lived Vinson's geckos, green as grass, with blue and scarlet heads.

I paused in the shade of a moderate-sized Latania to have an orange, and was treated to a very curious sight, which showed me how many Vinson's geckos a palm could support, and also what a predatory nature the Telfair's skink possessed.

I was sitting there, joyfully sucking my orange, when I heard a pattering noise on the leaves above me. I thought we were having a shower of rain, and it was raindrops I could hear on the stiff, cardboard-like fronds. The pattering went on, however, and I suddenly realised that I could not see any rain, nor could I feel any. Curious, I looked up at the fronds above me. Each great, green hand was made transparent by the sun and so I could see, scuttling and jumping, a shadow play of Vinson's geckos. Sometimes, one would stop for a moment and peer round the edge of the frond, before rushing farther up the palm. There were easily forty of them, from fully adult specimens to fragile babies about an inch long. They leapt from frond to frond with the agility of frogs; they were all moving upwards and it was obvious that something was causing them to panic. It was an extremely pretty sight to see their little bodies in black silhouette, running and jumping across the screen of green leaves.

I peered into the depths of the Latania to see what was alarming this host of jewel-like geckos, hoping it might be a snake. There, making his way laboriously but methodically up the stem, was a large Telfair's skink. Every now and then, he would pause in his climb and glance up, his tongue flicking in and out of his mouth. Up above, the panic-stricken geckos leapt and scuttled and peered round the fronds, their shiny black eyes looking round and horror-stricken in their little coloured faces. The Telfair's slow, ponderous approach had something rather prehistoric about it. After watching for a bit I decided that he had terrified the fairy-like Vinson's quite enough, so I caught him and transported him some fifty feet away from the Latania. When I came back to finish my orange, all the geckos had settled down to bask in the sun and resume their small lives.

Half an hour later, a triumphant shout from Wahab informed us that we had captured our fourth snake. Again, it was a juvenile, but somewhat bigger than Zozo's. We made our way back to camp, well satisfied, and even the tintinnabulation of the Shearwaters that night could not damp our enthusiasm.

Next morning, we had only time for one more search, since the helicopter was due to arrive at noon. We went off into the palm grove but met with no success, and so returned to the gruelling task of humping all our equipment down the valley and on to the heat-shimmered helipad. We left the tent up for shade and kept three jerry cans of water intact, using the others to give ourselves a much-needed bath.

At a quarter past twelve, Wahab began to get restive. At twelve-thirty, he started pacing up and down outside the tent. When he organised something, he liked it to run smoothly. At half past one, we made some tea and congratulated ourselves on not having used up all the water. At half past two, Wahab took Zozo outside. They went up on to the blistering helipad and stood there, gazing hopefully at the dim, heat-haze-blurred mountains of Mauritius.

'Wahab's very annoyed,' said John. 'He likes things to be done properly.'

'I know,' I said, 'but what can we do? We could radio, I suppose.'

When Wahab came back, I suggested it. He thought for a bit, and then we took the tiny radio transmitter up on to the helipad and stood in a perspiring circle, trying to make it work.

'It's no good,' said John, at last, 'it's as dead as the Dodo.'

Wahab gave him a reproachful look. We trooped back to the tent, leaving the defunct radio on the helipad.

'Zozo looks really worried,' said John, in a whisper.

'Well, he has only recently been married,' I pointed out. 'It's a bit early to find himself turned into a Robinson Zozo.'

'I think he really imagines we've had it,' said John.

Zozo was sitting, moodily, under a palm tree nearby. I decided to lighten his gloom.

'Zozo,' I called.

'Yes, Mr Gerry?' he said, peering at me from under the brim of his solar topee, which made him look ridiculously like a green mushroom.

'It seems as if the helicopter is not coming to rescue us.'

'Yes, Mr Gerry,' he agreed, soulfully.

'Well,' I said, kindly, 'I wanted you to know that, by an overwhelming vote, we have decided to eat you first when the food runs out.'

For a moment, he stared at me, wide-eyed; then he realised it was a joke and grinned. Even so, it did little to relieve his gloom. Wahab prepared to go up on to the helipad for the twentieth time.

'I can't understand where they are,' said Wahab, irritably.

'Look,' I said, soothingly, 'why don't we have a cup of tea? Zozo, put the kettle on.'

Zozo, glad to have something to do, filled the kettle.

'You'll see,' I said to Wahab, 'the moment that kettle starts to boil, the helicopter will arrive.'

'How do you know?' asked Wahab.

'White man's magic,' I said solemnly, and he grinned at me.

Strangely enough, just as the kettle started to boil, we heard the drone of the approaching helicopter. Within half an hour, we had packed everything in and, in an indignant snowstorm of tropic birds, took off with our precious cargo of snakes and lizards lying in their cloth bags on our laps.

At my request, the pilot circled the island at low level. We saw its great humpback, bare and desiccated, and the edge of its crater, as if some giant sea monster had taken a bite out of its side, and the pathetic, thin belt of palms and Latanias running like a pale green half-moon round one side, and over it looming the great sheets of eroded tuff. It seemed incredible that even now, when the island was practically dead, it should provide a home for such a variety of creatures and plants, and even more incredible that six of them should be found nowhere else in the world.

As we rose higher and higher, and the island dwindled against the turquoise sea, I became determined that we must do everything we could to save it.

CHAPTER SEVEN

PINK PIGEON POSTSCRIPT

By 1975 the Black River project had a pair of Pink pigeons, the female of which David McKelvey reckoned was too old to breed, and two odd male birds. As there had been no breeding success by 1976, it was thought imperative that some more birds be caught to increase the captive breeding stock. The problem was that the entire flock of pigeons appeared to have vanished from the cryptomeria grove. Looking for thirty-five birds in that vast area of forest was a Herculean task. John and Dave spent many hours soaked to the skin, hopefully surveying various areas; but all searches were in vain. When they should have been in the cryptomerias, building their ridiculous nests, they were nowhere to be seen. This was extremely worrying. With the benefit of hindsight we now think that the two cyclones, which had forced us to abandon Round Island and had bogged us down for so many days, were responsible for retarding the breeding season. However, at the tail end of our final trip, the Pink pigeons suddenly returned to the cryptomeria grove and started to nest.

Since nothing had been done between 1975 and 1976 and it seemed most urgent that a reasonable breeding group should be established, both in Mauritius and in Jersey, I decided that, after we had returned to Jersey, John should return to try to capture more Pink pigeons for the captive breeding project at Black River and to procure a breeding nucleus for us here. So after we had returned to Jersey with our precious cargo of Round Island geckos and snakes, John had to prepare to go back to Mauritius once again.

When he got back, he went straight to the cryptomeria grove and found himself a suitable tree. From this vantage point he could survey most of the valley. He settled down to await the Pink pigeons. After three hours, he began to wonder whether the pigeons had once more moved out of the cryptomerias to some other area. Then, glancing about, he suddenly saw, in the tree next door to him, a Pink pigeon sitting on a nest. As he said, 'Once I'd seen the damn thing, it was obvious that I had been staring at it for three hours and it had been invisible.' Greatly excited, he climbed down, made his way to the base of the tree with the nest in it, and sat there until dark to make sure that no monkeys found it, for he could hear troops of them all around in the forest.

When it was dark, he hurried back and alerted Wahab, Tony Gardner and Dave. The four of them planned to return to the nest at dawn. If there was a baby in the nest, they proposed to take it and replace it with a young rammier pigeon of the same size. Then they planned to put mist nets round the tree to catch the parent birds. All worked very well. They found to their delight that the nest contained an almost fully-fledged baby and this was duly replaced with the baby rammier pigeon. Then, with great difficulty, they rigged up the mist nets.

However, when the mother bird returned, either by cunning or stupidity – one suspects the latter – she evaded the nets but happily continued to feed a baby which in no way resembled her own. They waited all day but without success and so, leaving the nets in position, they went home to return the following morning at dawn. By the time they got back, monkeys had found the nest. It had been destroyed and the rammier chick devoured. So, although they could not catch the parent birds, at least they had the satisfaction of knowing that they had saved the Pink pigeon baby from being killed. It was kept in the aviaries at Black River and within three days was flying and feeding itself.

Meanwhile, John continued to search for nests, and soon discovered another one containing an egg. He and Dave had discussed at length what they should do in a case like this and had decided on a course of action. From Dave's observations they knew that both the sexes incubated the eggs and that the change-over between the parents occurred at 10 a.m. and 4 p.m. approximately. So the plan was to take the egg, to be placed eventually in the incubators at Black River, and to substitute for it a domestic pigeon's egg. Then the nest was to be covered with a specially adapted *bàl-chatri* in the hopes of catching the parents. By this means we would know that we had secured a true pair, for since the sexes were alike, if you caught an odd bird it was difficult to know what sex it was. The *bàl-chatri* is a very ancient device used by falconers for capturing hawks. It consists of a rounded cage, like an old-fashioned meat or cheese safe, into which is put one's bait – in the case of hawks, a bird and in the case of the nest, an egg. The whole of the top of the contrivance is covered with fine nylon nooses. The idea is that, once the bird lands on the *bàl-chatri*, it will get its feet entangled in one or other of the hundreds of little nooses that cover it.

In due course, Dave climbed the tree and replaced the egg with a domestic pigeon's egg. Then he carefully positioned the *bàl-chatri* over the whole nest. During this process the male pigeon had sat some thirty feet away and, according to John, showed no alarm and only a mild interest in what was happening. As soon as Dave had climbed down, the bird flew over and sat in the tree; it wandered about the branches, twice walking over the *bàl-chatri*. The third time, however, it was caught. They could hear it flapping frantically. David shinned back up the tree like lightning and captured the flapping bird only just in time, for it had been caught by only one toe. They waited two hours; then the female returned to the nest and was also caught within a very short time. In triumph, they transported the first known true pair of Pink pigeons to Black River.

Elated by the success of this method of capture, they decided on a concentrated search for more nests. With the addition of Zozo and two others to their numbers, they proceeded to comb the woods and within a week had tracked down four occupied nests. Out of this number, they managed to procure two more true pairs, and an odd female to join the two odd males at Black River.

Out of the eggs in the nests, one was found to be addled but on the morning that John left for Mauritius two of the others were successfully hatched under domestic pigeons and another hatching was awaited. This means that now, with seven adult specimens, the Black River project is viable, with enough Pink pigeons to ensure the captive breeding of the species.

John returned to Jersey with two pairs and an odd youngster. They have settled down remarkably well. This now means that, while the search for a solution to the problems of the monkeys and the preservation of the cryptomeria grove goes ahead, we hope that in Black River and in Jersey we will successfully breed a big enough population, protected from monkeys and cyclones alike. Eventually we will be able to return progeny to Mauritius to reinforce the tiny handful of wild birds left in their precarious habitat.

TAILPIECE

After our efforts to help so many endangered species, it is nice to be able to report that we have had breeding successes already. The Rodrigues bats have given birth to two fine healthy babies who are, at the time of writing, fully fledged, if you can use that term for a bat. The Telfair's skink and the Gunther's geckos from Round Island have hatched out seven and eleven babies respectively as have the phelsumas. We hope it won't be too long before we can also report success with the Round Island boas and the Pink pigeons. We are particularly pleased that, as the symbol of our Trust is the Dodo, we are able to help so many other endangered species from the island of Mauritius from which the Dodo was exterminated.

If you have read this book and enjoyed it and if you believe that the work we are doing for these gravely endangered species is of importance then I hope you will join our Trust. The subscription is modest but you will be helping work of enormous importance to many vanishing species.

With your help we can accelerate our efforts to help the extraordinarily bizarre and lovely creatures that I have described in this book, not only from Mauritius but from many different parts of the world.

AFTERWORD

by Toni Hickey, Senior Bird Keeper,
Durrell Wildlife Conservation Trust

I never expected the life of a bird keeper at the headquarters of the Durrell Wildlife Conservation Trust in Jersey to be a glamorous one, and the predicament I found myself in adequately illustrated this point. Phrases such as 'character building' sprang to mind as I scrambled in an undignified manner up a very imposing and slippery tree on the island of Mauritius. As I maneuvered myself higher, branch by branch, with all the grace and coordination of an under-tens baton twirlers club performing to a particularly jazzy and unfamiliar version of 'When the Saints Come Marching In', it occurred to me that perhaps I wasn't entirely equipped for life 'in the field'.

However, this was 'Annabelle', the very tree that Gerald Durrell mentions in this book, and climb it I most certainly would. So here I was, some twenty years later, retracing his footsteps, albeit with rather less joie de vivre. My own particular happiness derived from the fact that I had not yet not fallen out of the tree and landed on my own recently sharpened machete! My quarry, and reason for making such a spectacle of myself, was the pink pigeon.

Leaving a cloud of angry mosquitoes to regroup and plan their next assault at the foot of the tree, I finally reached the top. Well, when I say top, I mean a strategically placed viewing platform that a couple of dedicated/deranged Durrell-inspired fieldworkers had built. The idea behind this intrepid feat of amateur carpentry was to enable pigeon observations to be carried out with all the comfort and safety offered by a small wooden platform balanced precariously at the wobbly end of a 40 ft tree. But here I was, perched atop, and the view that swept down below me was breathtaking. Ahead, the forest sloped gently away into a gully, framed on either side by mountains which seemed to strain in their attempt to pin back the swollen, grey clouds. In the distance, the azure blue of the Indian Ocean draped the horizon like a blanket. However, something was missing...

Almost on cue, I heard a familiar call. The unmistakable 'bow coo' of a male pink pigeon, and a very handsome specimen he was too. With disdain, he surveyed me from a nearby tree. Presumably having established in his pigeon mind that I was neither a threat (male pink pigeon) nor a bit of the other (female pink pigeon) and consequently of no interest whatsoever, he proceeded to go about his business, whatever that was. Despite his indifference, that was a very special moment for me. Inspired by Gerald Durrell and the 'Ark' he created, I have made Jersey my home and have been working with birds at the Durrell Wildlife Conservation Trust (formerly Jersey Wildlife Preservation Trust) for four years, assisting with the conservation of this and many other species threatened with imminent extinction.

Our work came just in time for the pink pigeon, whose numbers had declined to disastrously low levels. Under the careful protection and management of our team in Mauritius, the pink pigeon is now safe and doing well. The population has grown from ten birds to over 350 in the forests of this unique island. Information gathered in Jersey about its health, nutritional needs, social behaviour and breeding habits has proved invaluable in overcoming problems and safeguarding the future of the pigeons.

However, it is not just the pink pigeon that has benefited from such intervention. Astonishing success has also been achieved with the Mauritius kestrel. This exquisite bird was reduced to only four known individuals in 1974, and many thought it couldn't be saved. Thankfully, due to a conservation effort led by the Trust's Carl Jones and spanning over twenty-five years, the population now stands at over 800 birds. The Rodrigues fruit bat mentioned in this book is yet another example. Through careful management, the wild population now numbers around four thousand. This has been achieved through management of their forest habitat and a public education campaign to eliminate hunting.

Back in 1984, Gerald Durrell (with the help of John Hartley and others) was instrumental in forming the Mauritian Wildlife Foundation: its purpose to conserve the threatened native flora and fauna of Mauritius, Rodrigues and their surrounding islets. The species I have mentioned were brought back from the brink of extinction with recovery programmes instigated and executed in Mauritius, and backed up by the support and expertise in Jersey.

Our joint efforts have had far-reaching effects. Our work with the endangered Mauritian birds galvanised the people of Mauritius into being more aware of and concerned about their special island wildlife. So much so that the Black River Gorges area in which we were working was designated a National Park by the government. In fact, Yousouf Mungroo, the very first graduate of Durrell Wildlife's International Training Centre in Jersey, became the first Director of the first National Parks in Mauritius. This training centre in Jersey is a highly respected facility where people from all over the world, including many among our Mauritian team, come to learn good conservation practice which they can then take back and apply in their own country.

So what of the reptiles taken from Round Island, I hear you ask? Having been comfortably installed in the 'Ark' for over twenty-five years with great success, the skink and gecko have now been retired back to Mauritius into semi-wild conditions (I am secretly hoping that this may happen to me one day). This leaves only the Round Island boa to update you on. We have made great inroads into understanding this enigmatic snake, but it has not completely revealed its secrets to us. There is still much to learn and the study in Jersey continues to help us to address conservation questions that would be difficult to undertake in situ.

So, I contemplated, perhaps even from this very spot Gerald Durrell's dream of a conservation effort to encompass a whole spectrum of rare and endangered species was formed. I allowed myself a brief moment of pride, and, I admit, a little smugness. But one must not rest upon one's laurels (especially when one is clinging to a gently swaying tree) for there is still much to be done. The Durrell Wildlife Conservation Trust continues to work with the pink pigeon both in the wild and, now in a largely ambassadorial role, in Jersey. More recently, the plight of the beautiful emerald echo parakeet, the rarest parakeet in the world, has also been addressed with a successful recovery programme in Mauritius. Over thirty years of conservation expertise on the island of Mauritius means that this inquisitive and bright little bird is in very safe hands.

Exciting new projects are constantly in development, with specialists from Jersey being sent to work alongside our local Mauritian staff. In fact, a colleague of mine will be trading a cold, wet Jersey winter for the blue skies of Mauritius as he helps to establish a recovery programme for a very delicate, rare and beautiful 'passerine' (that's a little songbird to the non-birdy experts among you).

Since this book was written, the restoration of Round Island has gone from strength to strength, with native plants being grown and translocated onto the island and, most recently, with the construction of a field station – much to the delight of the weather-beaten warden. Even the Aldabran giant tortoise has been seconded into a bit of manual labour for the greater good. On another island this close relative of the native Mauritian giant tortoises (hunted to extinction over a century and a half ago), has been found to be an excellent grazer of exotic, unwanted plants, leaving valuable native plants to grow undisturbed – much like a selective, benign, lumbering, lawn mower. If trials are successful this tortoise will soon be utilised on Round Island.

As the first few droplets of rain fell from the sky and clung gently to the forest grime that had already laid claim to my face, I realised that the time for reflection had passed and I ought to get moving. Limited experience of the tropics told me that these droplets do not usually travel in ones and twos, and so I would be wise to begin my descent before the mountains gave up their valiant struggle to hold back the clouds. I could imagine my mosquito welcoming committee in the vegetation below tutting and looking at their watches. I felt a mixture of emotions as I looked out over the forest for one last time: a great sense of pride at what had been achieved, a tinge of sadness that human impact invariably causes such damage, but mostly an enormous sense of hope and excitement for the future. Durrell Wildlife Conservation Trust, as part of its ongoing commitment to saving species worldwide, will continue to support the efforts of the Mauritian Wildlife Foundation in its endeavours to protect and propagate the animals and plants of this unique environment. And talking of another unique environment, the keepers and staff on site in Jersey will carry on investing our skill and expertise in caring for the precious animals entrusted to us by the government and people of Mauritius.

A MESSAGE FROM THE DURRELL WILDLIFE CONSERVATION TRUST

What Gerald Durrell did for the golden bat and the pink pigeon subsequently saved several native Mauritian species and inspired the founding of the country's first national park. His experiences with these animals gave fresh impetus and new inspiration to his lifetime crusade to preserve the rich diversity of animal life on our planet.

The crusade to preserve endangered species did not end with Gerald Durrell's death in 1995. His work goes on through the untiring efforts of the Durrell Wildlife Conservation Trust.

Over the years many readers of Gerald Durrell's books have been so motivated by his experiences and vision that they have wanted to continue the story for themselves by supporting his Wildlife Conservation Trust. We hope that you will feel the same way today because through his books and life, Gerald Durrell set us all a challenge. 'Animals are the great voteless and voiceless majority' he wrote, 'who can survive only with our help.'

Please don't let your interest in conservation end when you turn this page. Write to us now and we'll tell you how you can be part of our crusade to save animals from extinction.

For further information, or to send a donation, write to:

Durrell Wildlife Conservation Trust
Les Augrès Manor
Jersey
Channel Islands
JE3 5BP
Via UK

Or visit the website:

www.durrell.org